The Blackbirch Visual Encyclopedia

The Natural World

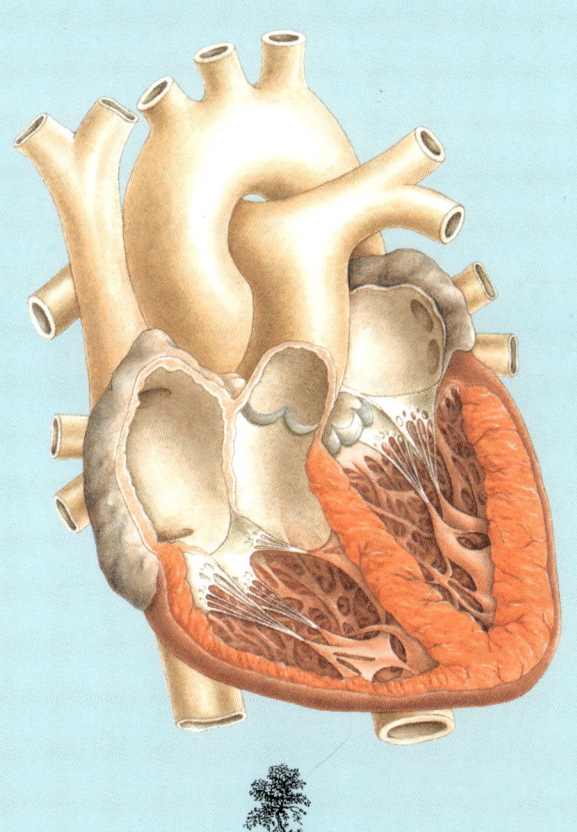

BLACKBIRCH® PRESS

THOMSON

GALE

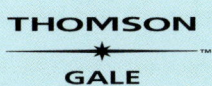

San Diego • Detroit • New York • San Francisco • Cleveland • New Haven, Conn. • Waterville, Maine • London • Munich

CONTENTS

THOMSON
GALE

© 2002 by Blackbirch Press™. Blackbirch Press™ is an imprint of The Gale Group, Inc., a division of Thomson Learning, Inc.

Blackbirch Press™ and Thomson Learning™ are trademarks used herein under license.

For more information, contact
The Gale Group, Inc.
27500 Drake Rd.
Farmington Hills, MI 48331-3535
Or you can visit our Internet site at http://www.gale.com

Copyright © 2000 Orpheus Books Ltd. Created and produced by Nicholas Harris, Joanna Turner, and Claire Aston, Orpheus Books Ltd.

ALL RIGHTS RESERVED
No part of this work covered by the copyright hereon may be reproduced or used in any form or by any means—graphic, electronic, or mechanical, including photocopying, recording, taping, Web distribution or information storage retrieval systems—without the written permission of the copyright owner.

Every effort has been made to trace the owners of copyrighted material.

Text credit: Steve Parker BSc Scientific Fellow of the Zoological Society

Illustration credit: Susanna Addario, Mike Atkinson, Graham Austin, Andrew Beckett, John Butler, Martin Camm, Malcolm Ellis, Simone End, Elisabetta Ferrero, Giuliano Fornari, Andrea Ricciardi di Gaudesi, Ian Jackson, Janos Marffly, Shane Marsh, Malcolm McGregor, Lee Montgomery, David More, Nicki Palin, Andie Peck, Alessandro Rabatti, Eric Robson, Claudia Saraceni, Peter David Scott, Richard Tibbits, Mark Wilkinson, Debra Woodward, Martin Woodward, David Wright

Photographs on page 53: Alex Bartel/Science Photo Library; on page 58: The Illustrated London News Picture Library

LIBRARY OF CONGRESS CATALOGING-IN-PUBLICATION DATA

Harris, Nicholas, 1956-
The natural world / Nicholas Harris.
    p. cm. — (Blackbirch visual encyclopedia)
    Summary: A visual encyclopedia of living things on Earth, including plants, animals, and humans, particularly looking at animal survival and the organs and systems of the human body.
    ISBN 1-56711-516-0 (lib. bdg. : alk. paper)
    1. Evolution (Biology)—Juvenile literature. 2. Life—Origin—Juvenile literature. [1. Evolution (Biology)—Encyclopedias. 2. Plants—Encyclopedias. 3. Animals—Encyclopedias. 4. Body, Human—Encyclopedias.] I. Blackbirch Press. II. Series.

QH367.1.N28 2002
570'.3—dc21   2002018662

Printed in Singapore
10 9 8 7 6 5 4 3 2 1

CONTENTS

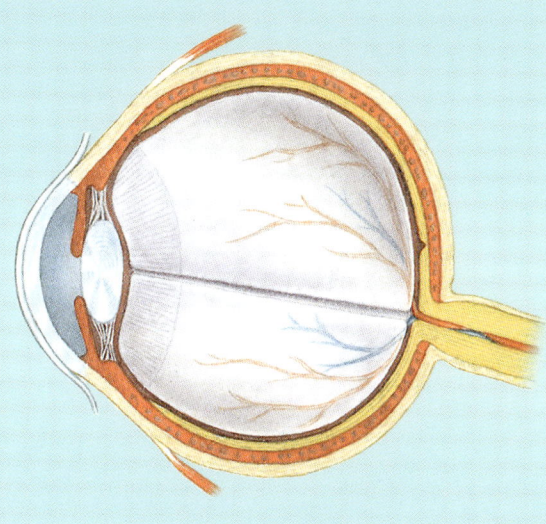

LIVING THINGS

4 WHAT IS LIFE?
Characteristics of an organism • Origins of life • Classification of living things

6 EVOLUTION
Evidence for evolution • Natural selection

8 BACTERIA
Recycling nutrients in the soil

9 VIRUSES • PROTISTS

PLANTS

10 PLANTS
Nonflowering plants • Flowering plants • Monocotyledons and dicotyledons

12 HOW PLANTS LIVE
Structure • Photosynthesis • Flowers and pollen • Pollination

14 SEEDS AND FRUITS
Seed dispersal • Germination

15 FUNGI
Life cycle of a toadstool

16 TREES
Broad-leaves and conifers • Layers of a tree trunk • How a tree lives • A tree's year

ANIMAL BIOLOGY

18 ANIMAL FEEDING
Characteristics of animals • Mouths • Food • Predators and parasites

20 ANIMAL SENSES
Hearing and vision • Smell and taste • Sensing electricity

22 MOVEMENT
Moving in water, in air, and on land

ANIMAL SURVIVAL

24 ADAPTATION
Adapting to hot and cold climates

26 ATTACK

27 DEFENSE
Spines and poisons

28 BEHAVIOR
Courtship • Territories • Helping others

30 MIGRATION
Birds • Insects • Ocean wanderers

HUMAN BODY

32 HUMAN BODY
Organs and systems

34 DIGESTION I
Inside the mouth • Teeth • Esophagus and stomach

36 DIGESTION II
Small intestine, liver, and kidneys

37 NUTRIENTS
Proteins, carbohydrates, and fats • Vitamins and minerals • Fiber

38 BREATHING
Respiratory system • Breathing rate • Cleaning the lungs • Speech

40 HEART

41 BLOOD
Arteries and veins • Circulatory system • Composition of the blood

42 MUSCLES • SKELETON

44 MUSCLES
How muscles work • Muscles in action

45 SKIN

46 BONES AND JOINTS
Characteristics of bones • Types of joints • Inside a joint • Fractures

48 THE BRAIN
Inside the brain • Nerve cells and signals • The nervous system

50 THE SENSES
Sight • Hearing • Taste • Smell

51 HORMONES

52 CELLS AND GENES
Inside a cell • How DNA multiplies

54 REPRODUCTION
Male and female sex organs • The first week of life • Cell division

56 A BABY GROWS
Early development • Life in the womb

58 MEDICINE
Medical and surgical treatment • Clean conditions • Doctors and hospitals • Emergency medicine

60 GLOSSARY

62 INDEX

Living things

WHAT IS LIFE?

LOOK AT your surroundings. There may be walls, windows, chairs, tables, and similar objects around you. Perhaps there are also machines, cars, and gadgets. There may be other people too, and pets and plants. Which ones are alive? You can probably tell at a single glance if an object is living or not. For example, a dog is alive but a book is not.

But exactly how did you decide which things are alive and which are nonliving? Perhaps you watch them to see if they move. A person or animal moves. Even a sleeping cat breathes softly. But a toy electric car moves and it is not alive, while a plant does not seem to move yet it is a living thing. Perhaps you look for signs of breathing. But the snails and plants in an aquarium do not seem to breathe, and they are alive. The giant panda *(above, right)* is just a picture, but you know from looking at it that a real panda would be alive. How?

Living things are called organisms. We know if something is a living organism, rather than nonliving, from several features. First, an organism grows and develops at some stage, usually changing its shape and getting bigger. Second, life processes happen inside the organism that change chemical substances from one form to another and which use up energy. Third, an organism must take in raw materials for its growth and also take in energy to power its life processes. Fourth, an organism reproduces—it produces more of its own kind.

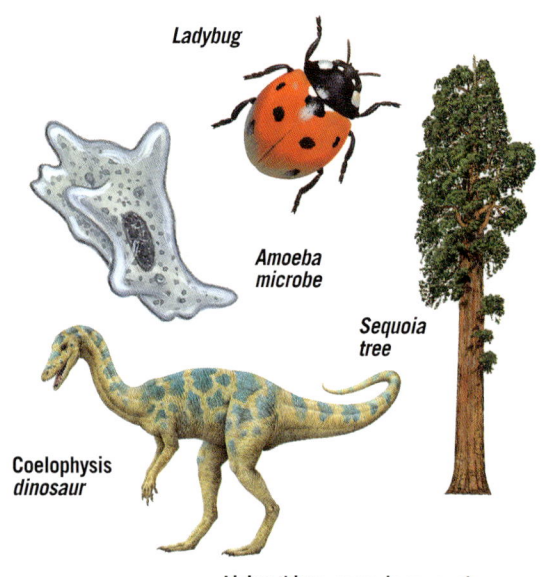

Ladybug

Amoeba microbe

Sequoia tree

Coelophysis dinosaur

Human being

Living things come in many shapes and sizes. Some are too small to see without a microscope, like an amoeba in the mud. Some are quite small and seen better with a magnifying lens, like a ladybug. Some are gigantic, like the sequoia tree. Some, like the dinosaurs, lived in prehistoric times but no longer survive. We humans are also living things.

LIVING THINGS

ORIGINS OF LIFE

How did life begin? Scientific studies show that planet Earth formed about 4,600 million years ago, from a massive ball of cloud, dust, and gases whirling through space. At first, the rocks of Earth were far too hot for life. But gradually they cooled and massive rainstorms lasting many thousands of years filled the lakes, seas, and oceans with water.

These seas contained all kinds of salts, minerals, and other chemical substances. By chance, some of them joined to each other—perhaps helped by the energy of lightning flashes from the storms that raged across the globe. A few simple chemicals gathered as blobs. Other chemicals joined around them. These others then broke off to form blobs of their own. The first very simple living things had reproduced. This may have happened as long as 3 billion years ago. Life stayed as simple microscopic organisms for another 2 billion years.

Did life come to Earth from outer space? Perhaps small, simple organisms arrived here on a meteorite or comet. They would have to be incredibly tough to withstand the extreme cold and harmful rays of space. Also this does not solve the question of life's origins. It must have started somewhere else!

The early Earth was a hostile, lifeless place. Volcanoes poured out red-hot molten rocks and poisonous fumes. Gigantic storms flooded the new land causing vast clouds of ash, spray, and steam. But over tens of millions of years, conditions cooled. The warm, shallow seas were a "primeval soup" of many chemicals, from which simple living things would form.

GROUPS OF LIVING THINGS

To understand how living things have changed or evolved in the past, and how they work and survive today, it helps to know which ones are similar to each other. So organisms are classified or put into groups. There were once only two main groups or kingdoms, plants, and animals. In modern science there are five, shown below.

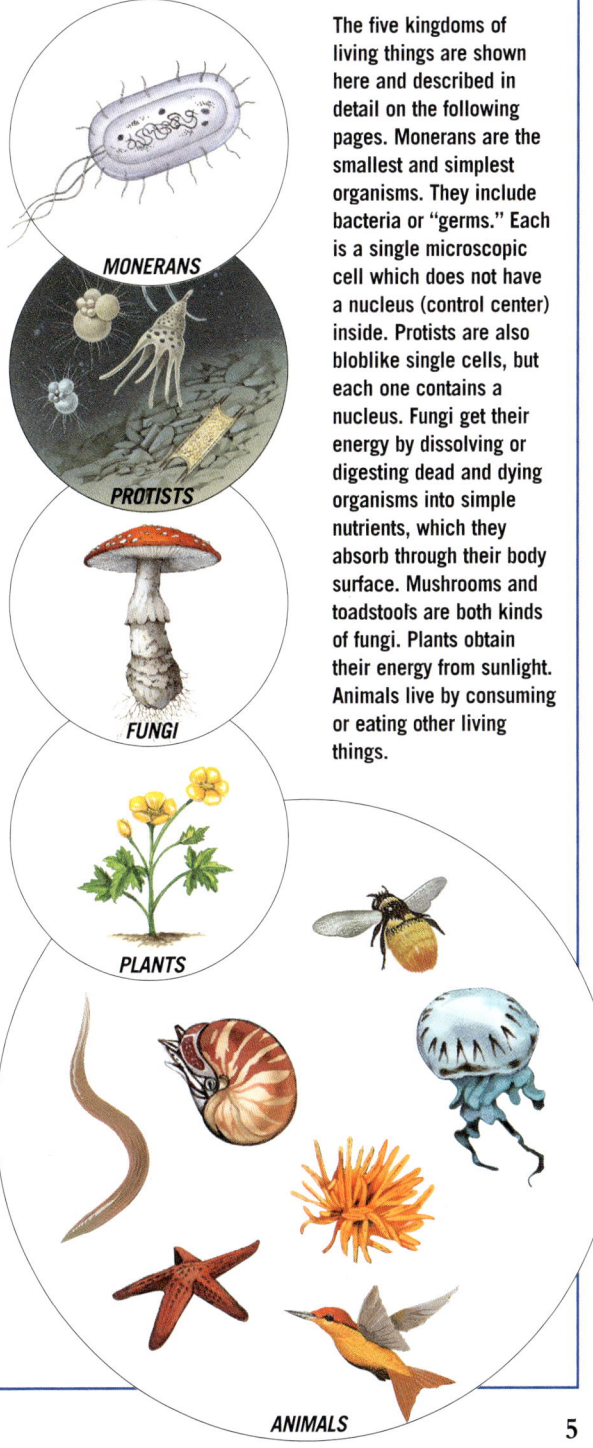

The five kingdoms of living things are shown here and described in detail on the following pages. Monerans are the smallest and simplest organisms. They include bacteria or "germs." Each is a single microscopic cell which does not have a nucleus (control center) inside. Protists are also bloblike single cells, but each one contains a nucleus. Fungi get their energy by dissolving or digesting dead and dying organisms into simple nutrients, which they absorb through their body surface. Mushrooms and toadstools are both kinds of fungi. Plants obtain their energy from sunlight. Animals live by consuming or eating other living things.

5

LIVING THINGS

EVOLUTION

A FOSSIL comes from an organism (living thing) that survived long ago. After the organism died, parts of it were buried in sand or mud, preserved in the rocks, and turned to solid stone. Hard, tough body parts form the best fossils because they do not rot away quickly after death and so have a better chance of being preserved. They include animal bones, teeth, horns, claws, and shells, and plant wood, bark, and cones.

Fossils show that many kinds of animals, plants, and other organisms have lived during the hundreds of millions of years that make up the earth's past. Most of these organisms, such as ammonites, trilobites, dinosaurs, and mammoths, are no longer alive. Other types have survived almost unchanged for millions of years. Sharks and turtles are examples of these. Some have appeared quite recently, such as human beings. The study of fossils, known as paleontology, is one part of the evidence for evolution—the way that living things change through time.

Why does evolution happen? Why don't living things simply stay the same? Life is a continual struggle to avoid predators and bad weather, to find food and shelter, and to breed. Living things that survive the struggle are those best suited or adapted to the conditions. However, the conditions change naturally with time. Some kinds of food may become more scarce. The climate may become colder or warmer. New diseases may appear. Living things must evolve to suit new conditions or die out.

The pink orchid mantis has evolved to resemble its flower and so be less noticed by prey.

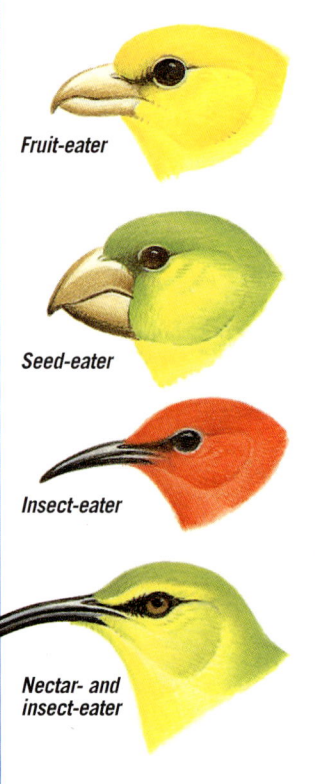

Fruit-eater

Seed-eater

Insect-eater

Nectar- and insect-eater

There are 28 different kinds or species of finches on the Hawaiian Islands. They are similar in general size, differing mainly in beak shape. Where did they come from? The Hawaiian Islands began to form only about five million years ago. A small flock of finches (of a single species) may have crossed the wide ocean and landed there. With no similar birds present, they could eat many different foods, such as soft fruits, hard seeds, insects and flower nectar. Their beaks changed, or adapted, to obtain each food source. Some finches flew to other islands in the group, where they continued to adapt. Slowly, the single finch species evolved into many species.

Besides studying fossils, we can see evolution at work by observing living things today. Some types of animals are very similar to each other. Hawaiian finches *(see left)*, for example, differ only in small ways. They probably all evolved from one original species. Their beaks changed, or adapted, to eat different foods.

There are two living species of elephants, African and Asian. Fossils of huge bones, teeth, and tusks resembling those of today's species show that many other kinds of elephants once roamed the earth. Each type evolved to suit the conditions of its time, such as an ice age or a warm period. But it could not adapt as conditions continued to change and so died out.

Paleomastodon

Moeritherium

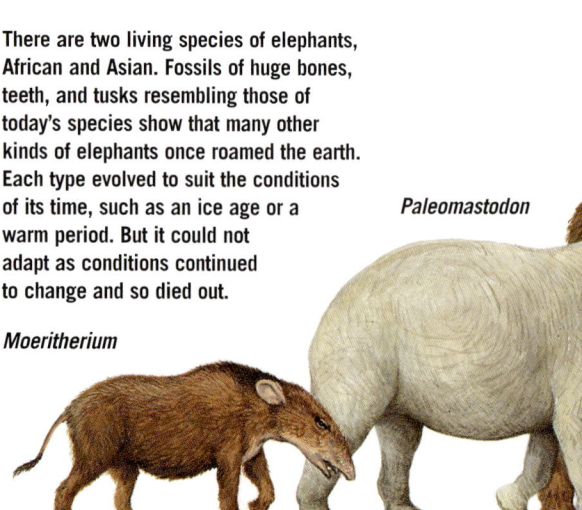

LIVING THINGS

The adult human body does not have gills or a tail, like a fish. But it does have these features for a short time in the very early stages of development, when it is an embryo. In fact the embryos of all vertebrate animals (those with backbones) look very similar to each other. This is because they have all evolved from the same distant ancestors.

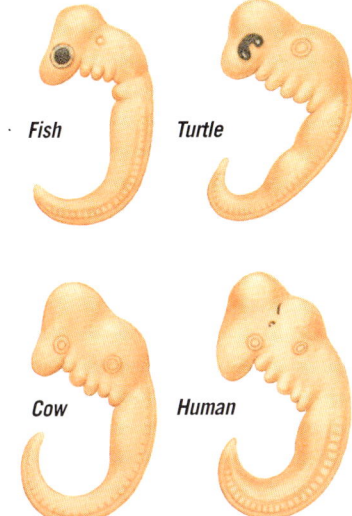
Fish *Turtle*
Cow *Human*

NATURAL SELECTION

Evolution happens by the process of natural selection. In the struggle for survival, some living things adapt better to the conditions. These individuals are more likely to survive and produce offspring. If the offspring inherit the same features, they too have more chance of survival. It is as if nature chooses who will survive and who will not.

EVIDENCE FOR EVOLUTION

An embryo is a living thing at an early stage of its development, like a human baby during the first few weeks of life growing in its mother's womb. At this early stage, a developing human embryo looks very similar to the embryo of any other mammal, such as a monkey or cow. It is also similar to the embryo of a bird, a reptile like a turtle, and even a fish. The simplest explanation as to why these very young organisms are so similar to each other is evolution. Over millions of years they have evolved from the same ancestors. They are now different as adults. But they have kept the similarities to their ancestors, and so to each other, during the early stages of their development.

A feature that helps an organism's success in breeding is encouraged or increased by evolution. The male bird of paradise's beautiful plumage makes him more attractive to females. This increases his chances of producing offspring with similar plumage. This aspect of evolution is known as sexual selection.

Bird of paradise

Evolution by natural selection explains the bodily features and behaviors of living things—even those that seem to be a hindrance. The long, colorful feathers of a male bird of paradise may seem a drawback. They make him more obvious to predators and less able to escape from them. But they also attract females for breeding, and so this feature is passed on to his offspring.

Gomphotherium *Steppe mammoth* *Modern African elephant*

LIVING THINGS

BACTERIA

THE MOST COMMON living things are bacteria. They are too small to see without a microscope. Most are about one to five microns (0.001 to 0.005 millimeters) across. A quarter of a million would fit on the head of a pin. Bacteria are all around us in their billions. They float in air and live on icy mountaintops, in the scalding water of hot springs, in dark caves, and at the bottom of the sea. There are more than 4,000 known kinds, and probably many more yet to be identified. They vary in form but there are three main shapes. These are: spheres or balls known as cocci, cylinders or rods, called bacilli, and corkscrewlike spirilli. Most bacteria reproduce simply by splitting in two.

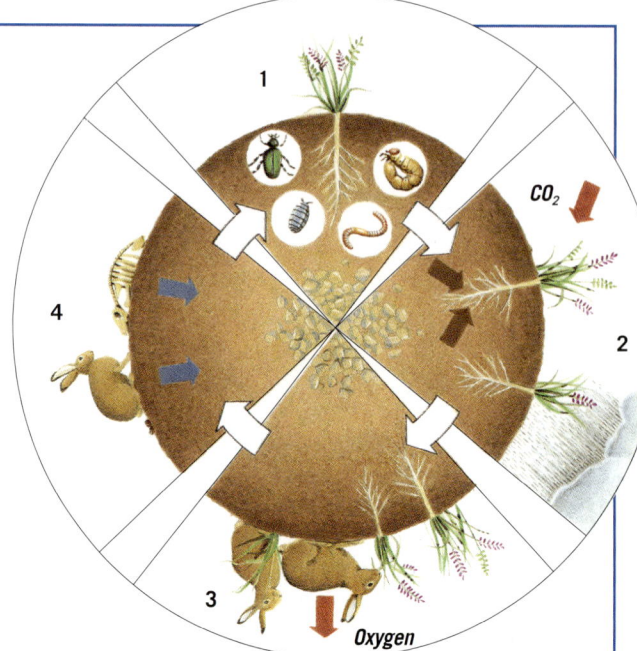

Bacteria and other microbes rot down and recycle nutrients in the soil (1). These nutrients are taken up by plants (2). The plants provide food for animals (3). Waste and dead animals decay, returning nutrients to the soil (4).

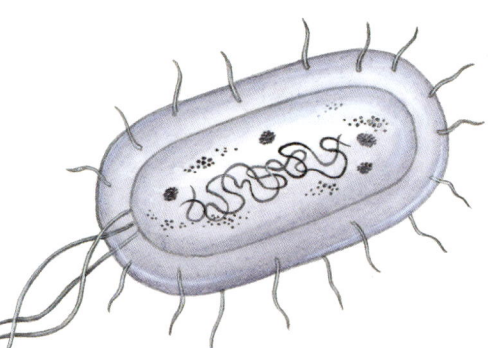

A bacterium is little more than a tiny bag of chemicals including DNA. Some kinds have a long, whiplike "tail," or flagellum.

Bacteria belong to the main kingdom of living things known as monerans *(see page 5)*. A typical bacterium has a tough outer skin, or cell membrane, which contains jellylike cytoplasm. Tiny blobs, known as ribosomes, float in the jelly and make various substances for the bacterium's life processes. Also floating in the cytoplasm is a long, coiled-up chemical called DNA, which unravelled would be more than 1,000 times longer than the bacterium itself. This is the bacterium's genes, a "manual" containing every structural detail of the organism. Some bacteria get their energy from light, like plants. Others absorb nutrients through their cell membranes.

Some bacteria are harmful. They get into other living things, including humans, and cause diseases such as anthrax and typhoid. But most bacteria are harmless. Many kinds live in the soil and play a vital role in nature because they cause the decay or rotting of dead plants and animals *(above)*.

Bacteria may get into the body through a cut or on a dirty object (1). White blood cells (2) gather at the site to attack them.

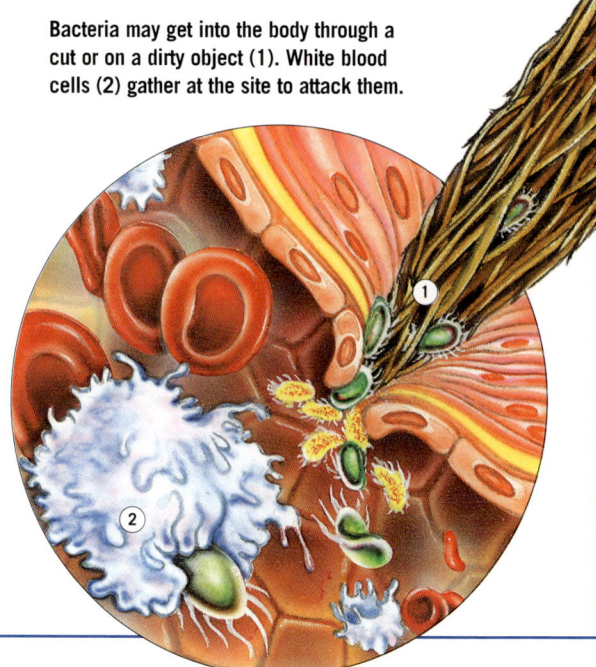

8

LIVING THINGS

VIRUSES

THE SMALLEST living things are viruses. They are "alive" only because they can produce more of their kind if they invade another living thing. Viruses cannot reproduce on their own. They get into another living cell *(see page 52)*, the host cell, and take over its life processes to make more copies of themselves. In the process they destroy the host cell.

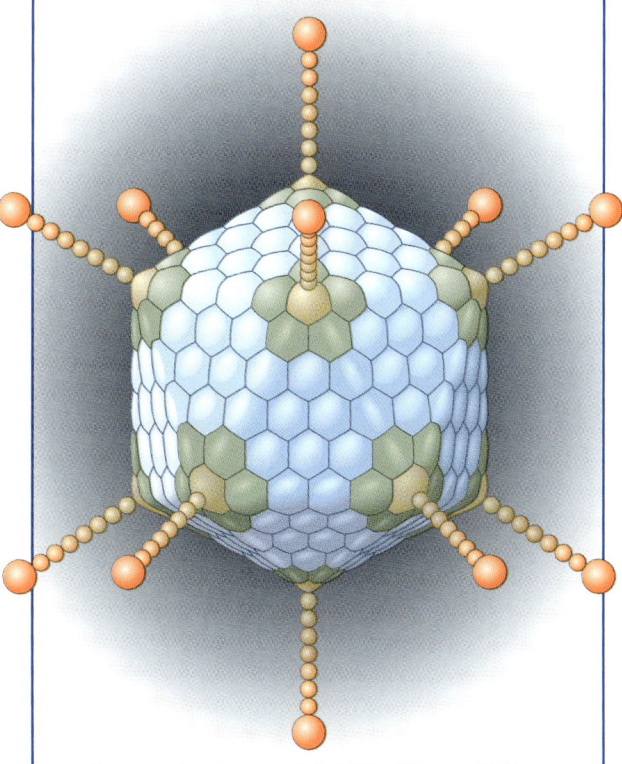

An adenovirus is so small that 10 million would fit on the period at the end of this sentence. This type of virus causes colds and flu. It has an outer protein shell made of triangular sections.

A typical virus has an outer shell or coat made of proteins. Inside is a length of genetic material, usually DNA. Different viruses are shaped like bricks, rods, golf balls, and even space rockets. Many can exist in their nonliving form for years and be frozen solid, boiled, or made into crystals—yet still come alive when host cells are available. Viruses cause diseases in plants, animals, and people. These include the common cold, measles, and AIDS (caused by the Human Immunodeficiency Virus, HIV).

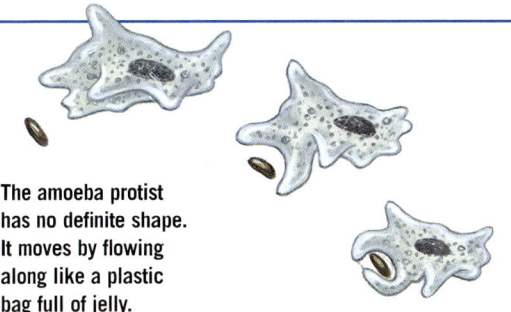

The amoeba protist has no definite shape. It moves by flowing along like a plastic bag full of jelly.

PROTISTS

LIKE BACTERIA and other monerans, protists are microscopic single cells. But unlike monerans, each protist has its genetic material (DNA) wrapped inside a baglike membrane to form the nucleus or control center of the cell. Protists live mainly in water and damp places. Some are like tiny plants, absorbing their energy from sunlight and their raw materials for growth from the water around them. Others move around and consume food particles such as bacteria.

Billions of protists live in the sea. As they die, their tiny shells sink and form the thick, muddy ooze on the sea bed.

Some protists have a rigid, caselike cell wall around them. The types known as foraminiferans and radiolarians *(above)* make shells with beautiful shapes and patterns. Others have no rigid case and can take up any shape. A few protists cause diseases, such as plasmodia, which produce malaria.

PLANTS

PLANTS

THE SECOND LARGEST kingdom of living things after animals is the plants. The key feature of a plant which sets it apart from other living things is that it obtains energy from light by the process of photosynthesis *(see page 12)*. Most plants have broad, flat surfaces, such as leaves or fronds, where this happens. Just as there are many groups of animals, from simple worms to complicated mammals, so there are many groups of plants. However, they are divided into two main kinds—the simpler types without flowers, and those with flowers.

Ferns can survive on low levels of light. Many types grow in woodlands in the shade under large trees.

The tiny plants that drift in the ocean, phytoplankton, are a mix of protists and small algae. They are food for tiny animals, zooplankton.

Some seaweeds grow to enormous sizes. Giant kelps have fronds more than 200 feet (61 m) long and in good conditions they can grow more than three feet each day. Like trees on land, they are food and shelter for many animals.

NONFLOWERING PLANTS

The simplest nonflowering plants are algae. They nearly all live in water, although a few kinds can survive in damp places, like *Pleurococcus* alga which grows as a green powder on shady tree trunks. Nearly all seaweeds and some types of pondweeds, such as the green, hairlike spirogyra, are algae. An alga has no proper roots, stem, or leaves, although it may have a stemlike part and leaflike blade. It absorbs water and nutrients through its body surface.

Mosses and liverworts are known as bryophytes. A moss has small green leaflets but no proper stem or roots. It absorbs water and nutrients through its leaflets so it can only live in damp places. Liverworts grow in similar places. Each has a low, flattened body known as a thallus.

Ferns, or pteridophytes, are also nonflowering. A fern has roots which absorb water and minerals from the soil, and a stiff stem to hold up its much-branched fronds. The stem, like the stem of a flowering plant, contains tiny pipes or tubelike vessels to carry the water and other substances from the roots to the fronds. Plants with these vessels are known as vascular plants.

All of these nonflowering plants reproduce by making tiny, dustlike spores which grow into new plants. Conifers, also called gymnosperms, reproduce by seeds. The seeds form in hard, scaly structures known as cones. Pines, firs, spruces, larches, redwoods, and cypresses are all conifers.

PLANTS

Giant sequoia

Magnolia

The first plants to evolve on Earth were probably small, simple seaweeds or algae. The first land plants grew some 400 million years ago. Conifer trees dominated the land from about 200 to 120 million years ago. Then the first flowers, similar to magnolias, appeared. Flowering plants soon took over the land.

FLOWERING PLANTS

The flowers of flowering plants, also known as angiosperms, are body parts specialized for breeding. The flowers produce seeds which in suitable conditions grow into new plants, as shown on the following pages. Flowering plants are by far the main or dominant group of plants around the world, except for seaweeds in the oceans and the conifer forests in colder regions. Flowering plants include familiar herbs, grasses, reeds, rushes, wild and garden flowers, and most trees and bushes (except for the conifers). There are some 260,000 different kinds or species of flowering plants compared to about 550 species of conifers, 11,000 ferns, 23,000 mosses and liverworts, and around 12,000 species of algae.

All conifers, or cone-bearing plants, are bushes or trees. Most have long, narrow leaves that do not fall off in autumn and so are known as evergreens. The biggest living things on Earth, giant sequoias weighing over 2,205 tons, are conifers.

Palms grow in dry, tropical lands. A date palm can grow up to 100 feet (30 m) high and live for 200 years.

Crocus

Buttercup

The two main kinds of flowering plants are named from the number of cotyledons. These are nutrient-packed "seed leaves" that provide food for the baby plant as it grows from a seed. Monocots have one cotyledon and include palms, grasses, and some flowers such as lilies, crocuses, and orchids. Dicots have two cotyledons and include all other kinds of flowers, bushes, and trees.

11

PLANTS

How Plants Live

A PLANT may not look lively and active. But inside its millions of microscopic cells, thousands of chemical changes take place as part of the plant's life processes. Like an animal's body, a plant's body has many specialized parts for different jobs. The roots take in water, minerals, salts, and other substances from the soil in which the plant grows. The stiff stem holds the main parts of the plant above the surface, away from animals on the ground that might eat it, and above other plants so that the leaves can catch more sunlight.

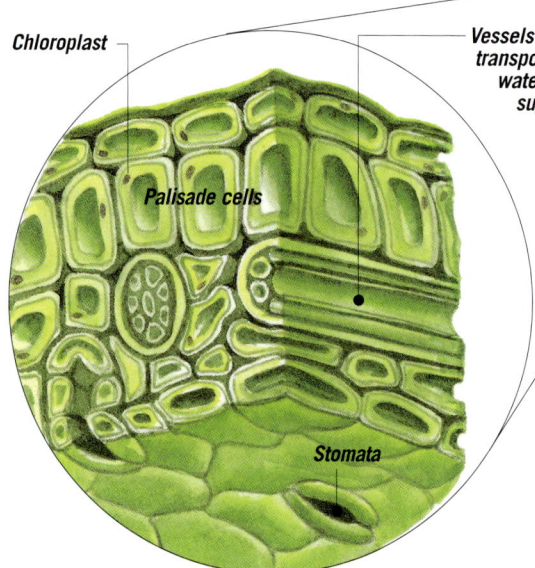

The tall palisade cells in the leaf's upper surface have many tiny blobs or discs called chloroplasts. These contain the chlorophyll that carries out photosynthesis.

A plant's leaves are "light-powered food factories." They are broad and flat so that as much light as possible falls on them. A green substance called chlorophyll in the leaves catches or absorbs the energy in light. It uses this energy to make a chemical reaction. Water, taken up from the soil, and carbon dioxide, taken in from the air, join together to form sugar, which contains lots of energy in chemical form. The plant then uses the sugar to power its life activities. The process is called photosynthesis—a word meaning "making with light."

The carbon dioxide for photosynthesis comes from the air. It seeps into the leaf through tiny holes in its lower surface, known as stomata. In addition to sugar, photosynthesis also produces oxygen, which seeps out into the air. Living things including ourselves need oxygen to survive. Plants help to top up its level in the air.

The Venus flytrap lives in poor soil with few minerals and nutrients. It catches small animals, dissolves them, and takes in their juices as an extra nutrient supply.

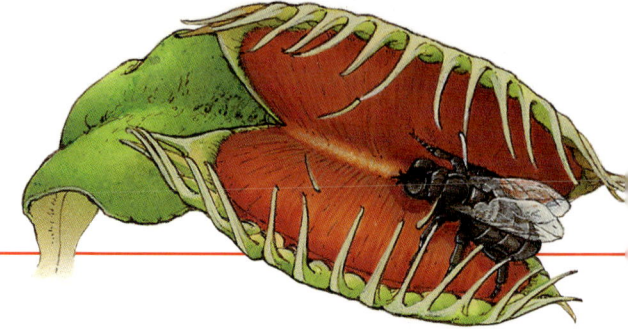

12

PLANTS

FLOWERS AND POLLEN

A plant's flower is designed to reproduce—make seeds which grow into new plants. A typical flowering plant has both male and female parts. The male parts make tiny particles, pollen grains, which look like fine yellow powder. Each grain contains a male cell. Pollen is produced in baglike anthers on stalks, called filaments. The female cells or ovules (eggs) are in the ovary, a fleshy part at the flower's base. A taller part, called the style, sticks up from this, with the stigma at its top. Pollen must travel from the anthers of one flower to the stigma of another of the same kind, so the male and female cells can join and develop into seeds.

Many different kinds of animals help to pollinate flowers. They include birds, insects, and various kinds of mammal. Like others, the honey Opossum comes to drink the flower's sweet nectar or "honey."

The transfer of pollen is called pollination. Some pollen grains are light and balloonlike and are blown by the wind. Others are sticky and carried by animals. To attract animals, the flower has colorful petals and a strong scent and makes a sugary liquid called nectar. When animals come to drink the nectar, the pollen sticks to them. It brushes off at the next flower onto the stigma. A tube grows from the pollen grain down the style to the ovary. The male cell moves down this to join the ovule.

A microscope shows grooves, spikes, and other structures on a pollen grain. Each kind of plant has its own pollen grain pattern.

FEMALE PARTS

Stigma

Style

Ovary (in flower base)

The reproductive parts of the flower are usually in the center. Some flowers have only male or female parts rather than both. The colorful petals attract animals such as insects to carry pollen.

MALE PARTS

Anther

Filament

Petal

13

PLANTS

SEEDS AND FRUITS

AFTER male pollen grains have been carried to the female parts of a flower *(see page 13)*, the male and female cells join and begin to develop into the baby plant. The flower parts are no longer needed and they shrivel away, to be replaced by the developing seeds in the seedhead. A seed is usually accompanied by a food store for its early growth, neatly packaged inside a casing. Some plants, like orchids, produce many thousands of tiny seeds. An ear of wheat is a head of wheat seeds or grains. We grind them up to make flour.

Fruits come in a wide variety of forms. The seeds are usually small and hard. They are known as pips in apples and oranges, kernels in nuts, and stones in berries like the cherry. However some seeds are soft and fleshy, like peas in their fruit, the pod.

Peas

Orange

Sweet chestnut

Cucumber

Sunflower

Walnut

Case   Seed

Cherry

FRUITS AND NUTS

A fruit is the protective case around a seed. Some fruits are very light, like the feathery "parachutes" of the dandelion. They blow away in the wind. Some fall into water and float to a new place, like the coconut. A nut has an especially tough outer case. Animals may crack some nuts and eat the seeds within, but they also drop many as they feed. A squirrel buries nuts such as acorns, but may forget to dig them up, so in effect it has planted new oak trees! Some fruits have juicy, tasty flesh. These are known by the everyday name of "fruits." The fruity part attracts animals to eat it. The seeds are spilled or pass through the animal's guts to emerge unharmed and far away.

Maple seed

Jay, a seed-eating bird

Hazel flicks out seeds

Squirrel, a seed-burying mammal

Seeds are spread or dispersed in many ways. The maple tree's winged seed twirls away in the wind. Birds and mammals may drop seeds in their dung.

Seeds have a better chance of growing if they are away from the parent plant. If they fall next to the parent, they would be in its shade and would also compete with it for soil nutrients. For these reasons, seeds have many ways of being spread far and wide.

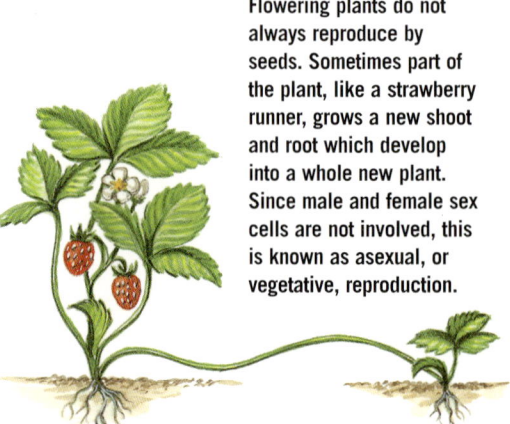

Flowering plants do not always reproduce by seeds. Sometimes part of the plant, like a strawberry runner, grows a new shoot and root which develop into a whole new plant. Since male and female sex cells are not involved, this is known as asexual, or vegetative, reproduction.

14

PLANTS

When a bean seed germinates, its main root probes down into the soil to absorb water and nutrients (1). The shoot arches up and straightens (2). The seed leaves open out and begin photosynthesis (3). The seed case falls away and the main shoot starts to lengthen (4).

A seed germinates, or begins to grow, only when conditions are suitable. This usually requires moisture of some kind, the right temperature, and perhaps darkness, which means the seed is buried in the soil. Some seeds like those of the ironwood tree do not germinate unless they have been scorched by fire. This usually means many plants have burned away so the ground is bare and ready for new life. Other seeds do not germinate until after they have been cracked by frost and then warmed slightly, that is, when winter is over and spring has arrived. When conditions are right, the baby plant begins to grow using its store of food in the seed leaves, or cotyledons. It splits its case, sends roots down into the soil and grows its shoot up toward the light.

The world's largest flower, the rafflesia of Southeast Asia, has no leaves, stem, or roots. It is a parasite. It steals ready-made nourishment by growing thin threads into another plant, such as a jungle vine.

FUNGI

MUSHROOMS, toadstools, brackets, yeasts, molds, and mildews are all fungi. They form one of the five great groups or kingdoms of living things. Fungi are rotters. They grow networks of thin, pale threads, called hyphae, into the bodies of dead and dying plants and animals. The threads cause the body to decompose. They then absorb the released nutrients through their surface. Like bacteria *(see page 8)*, fungi are nature's recyclers. They return the nutrients in dead animal and plant matter or animal droppings back into the soil.

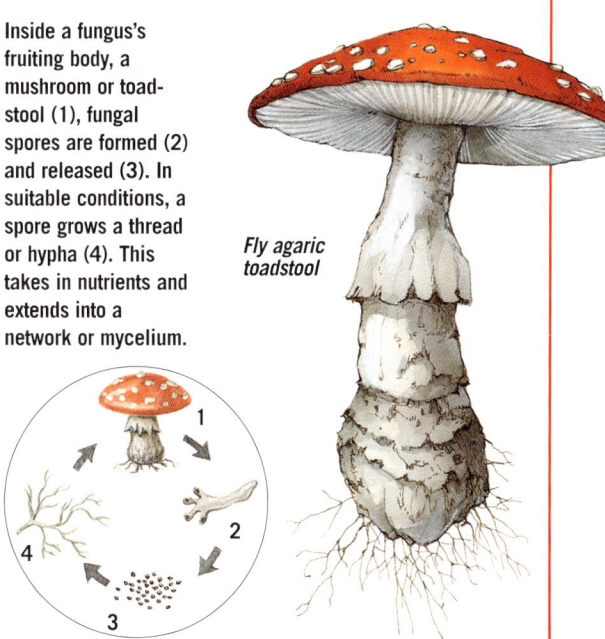

Inside a fungus's fruiting body, a mushroom or toadstool (1), fungal spores are formed (2) and released (3). In suitable conditions, a spore grows a thread or hypha (4). This takes in nutrients and extends into a network or mycelium.

Fly agaric toadstool

A fungus's network of threads is known as the mycelium. It is usually hidden in the soil, inside a dead animal's body or under a dying tree's bark. So we rarely notice fungi at work. We are more likely to notice them when they reproduce. They do this by growing fruiting bodies. Many of these are shaped like umbrellas—we call them mushrooms and toadstools. The presence of a mushroom indicates a network of hyphae in the soil below, rotting down and absorbing nutrients. The mushroom's top, or cap, releases millions of tiny fungal spores that blow away in the wind.

PLANTS

TREES

A TREE is a large plant with a woody stem or trunk, covered with a layer of bark. There are two main groups of trees: the broadleaves and the conifers. Broad-leaved trees are flowering plants that produce fruits with seeds inside. Conifers produce cones, which carry seeds on the face of each of their scales.

Many broadleaved trees are deciduous: their leaves drop in autumn, or, in hot countries, during the dry season. Some broadleaves and nearly all conifers are evergreen. Their leaves do fall, but not all at the same time. The palm tree, which grows in hot countries, is a different type of tree. It usually has no branches and only a few large leaves at its tip.

Trees are a valuable resource. They give us fuel, timber, medicines, food, paper, rubber and even soap. Even more importantly, they take in carbon dioxide and give off oxygen, so maintaining the balance of gases in the atmosphere.

A tree trunk has several layers. The outer bark protects against damage, cold and heat and water loss. Inside this is the inner bark, also known as the phloem. This carries all the food (types of sugar) that has been made in the leaves all around the rest of the tree. Next comes the growth layer of the tree. Inside that lies the sapwood, or xylem, which carries water from the roots up to the leaves. Finally, at the centre of the tree is a core of old sapwood called the heartwood. This gives the tree its strong "backbone".

Each year of a tree's life the growth layer of the trunk makes new bark on the outside and new sapwood on the inside. In this way, the trunk becomes thicker every year. If you look at the stump of a freshly cut-down tree, the sapwood that is added each year appears as a single ring. Count the number of rings and you will find the age of the tree.

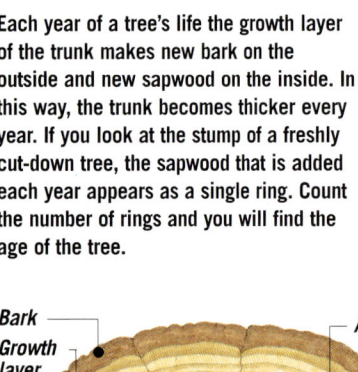

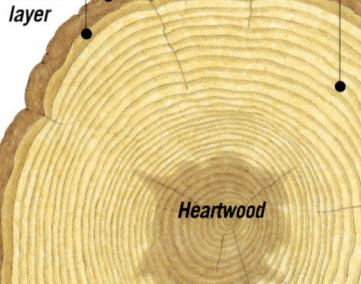

16

PLANTS

Leaf

Leaves have a network of veins which carry food and water, and support the rest of the leaf.

HOW A TREE LIVES

Like all plants, a broadleaved tree has roots and a shoot. The shoot is made up of a trunk (its stem) and branches bearing leaves buds and flowers. The trunk holds up the tree while the branches and twigs spread out the leaves so that they receive as much sunlight as possible. The leaves themselves grow in a spiral pattern to avoid shading those below. Water *(blue arrow)* is drawn up from the soil to the leaves through the sapwood. The leaves use the water and sunlight, as well as carbon dioxide in the air to make food by photosynthesis *(see page 12)*. This food *(red arrow)* passes from the leaves to all other parts of the tree through the inner bark.

At the base of the tree, a network of roots spreads outwards, anchoring it into the ground. Behind the root tips lie the root hairs which soak up water and nutrients from the soil. A large tree may take up several hundreds of litres of water every day.

A TREE'S YEAR

As spring arrives, the buds of the horse chestnut tree open, the shoots lengthen and the leaves unfold. Flowers blossom, ready for pollination *(see page 13)*. In summer, the leaves are fully open. The fruits, made up of a spiny casing with a large seed or "conker" inside, ripen and fall to the ground. During autumn, the leaves turn brown as food drains from them into the trunk. A scar forms at the base of each stalk and the leaves fall off. In winter, the tree is protected by its waterproof bark. The buds, next year's leaves and flowers, are covered by scales.

The banyan tree is a holy tree in India. Its roots grow downwards from its branches and support them like pillars. This allows the tree to keep growing outwards. One giant measured 600 metres around its circumference.

A conifer tree bears cones instead of fruit. Firs, pines, spruces and redwoods are all conifers. Most grow in colder lands. Many kinds, like this Douglas fir, have small, needle-like leaves.

17

ANIMAL BIOLOGY

ANIMAL FEEDING

OF THE FIVE great kingdoms of living things, the animal kingdom is by far the largest. Scientists have identified at least two million different kinds or species, from tiny worms smaller than a period, to huge elephants and blue whales. There are almost certainly at least the same number of species still to be identified—mainly insects in tropical forests. The total number of animal species may be far higher: 10 million, or even more. The key features of an animal are that it has a body made of many microscopic cells and it gets its energy and nutrients by eating—that is, it takes in or consumes food. Most animals can also move about during all or part of their lives.

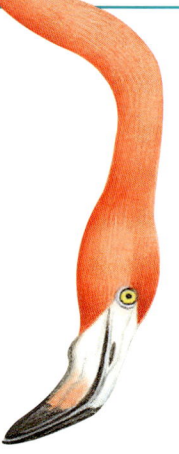

Many kinds of animals, from oysters and sea lilies to flamingoes and great whales, are filter-feeders. They filter, or sieve, small water organisms using a mouth equipped with hairs or flaps that make a brush- or comblike structure.

Butterflies and moths like this hawkmoth drink rather than eat. The mouth is a long tube normally coiled up, under the head. It straightens out like a drinking straw to dip into flowers and sip their nectar.

MOUTHS

There are almost as many different sizes and designs of animal mouth as there are different kinds of food. Most mammals like ourselves have teeth that can bite smaller pieces from a large food item and then chew the pieces into a soft pulp that is easily swallowed. But some mammals have few teeth—or none at all. The anteater collects its tiny food items of ants and termites by flicking out its long, sticky tongue. The vampire bat has front teeth like razor blades but it only uses them to slice a slit in its victim's skin. Then it uses its tongue to lap up its meal of blood.

Birds lack teeth, although they can peck powerfully with their strong, horn-covered beaks. Some birds have long, thin beaks like tweezers for probing into cracks or mud for small food items. Others have deep, short, powerful beaks that work like nutcrackers, for splitting seeds and nuts. Frogs also lack teeth for biting and chewing. They grab their food and gulp it down whole.

Most animals ingest their food. This means they take food items into their bodies through an opening, the mouth, to be digested and absorbed inside. However, a few creatures feed in more unusual ways. A tapeworm inside another animal's gut is surrounded by already-digested food. Also the tapeworm has no mouth. It simply soaks in or absorbs the nutrients through its very thin body surface.

The tiger is an ambush predator. It creeps close, charges the last few feet and kills with a neck bite.

ANIMAL BIOLOGY

Food

Most animals eat mainly plants or plant parts such as leaves, fruits, seeds, shoots, and roots. They are herbivores. Some animals eat mainly the flesh of other creatures (sometimes their whole bodies). They are called carnivores. Other animals eat a wide range of both plant and animal food and are known as omnivores. A few animals, like dung beetles and crabs, eat dead or rotting food and wastes. They are detritivores.

Lice are blood-sucking insects that live as parasites on larger animals. Different kinds infest various types of birds and mammals, like this human head louse.

Predators and Parasites

A predator is an animal that hunts down and catches its victims, known as the prey. Some predators are large and fierce, like lions, wolves, crocodiles, and sharks *(see page 26)*. Others are small but just as fierce, like shrews, newts, ragworms, and diving beetles.

A parasite is an organism that takes its nourishment or shelter from another, the host. It may harm the host in the process but does not necessarily kill it. Fleas, lice, ticks, and tapeworms are animal parasites. Mistletoe is a plant parasite of other plants.

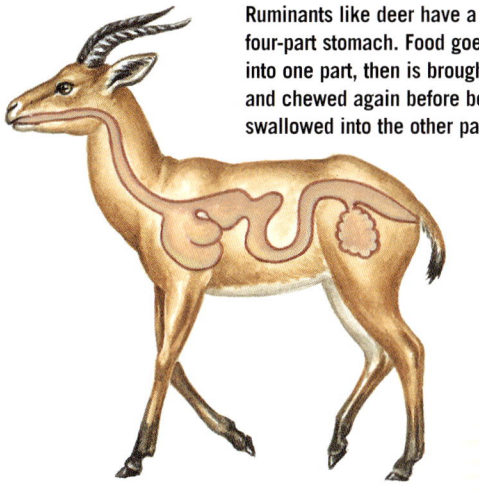

Ruminants like deer have a four-part stomach. Food goes into one part, then is brought up and chewed again before being swallowed into the other parts.

Food is broken down by the digestive system. This is usually a long tube coiled inside the animal's body. The first part is the baglike stomach with its muscular wall. It stores and squashes the meal. Next is the long intestine that absorbs the nutrients. Wastes pass out of the other end, the anus.

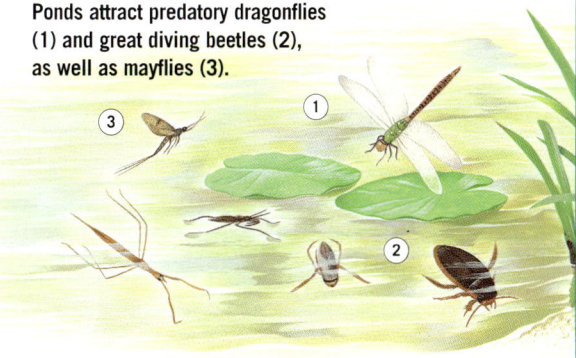

Ponds attract predatory dragonflies (1) and great diving beetles (2), as well as mayflies (3).

A few kinds of animals do not feed at all. A young mayfly leaves the water, splits its old skin and flies off as a winged adult. But it has no mouth and cannot eat. It mates and dies within a day.

ANIMAL BIOLOGY

ANIMAL SENSES

MOST ANIMALS move around as they search for food, shelter, or mates and avoid danger. So they have senses to detect what is going on around them. We have the same five main senses as many animals *(see page 50)*—sight, hearing, smell, taste, and touch. Our main sense is sight. Compared to many animals, our eyes see clearly, in detail, and in an especially wide range of colors. However, some animals have much better sight and other senses than we do. Some can even detect what we cannot, like tiny pulses of electricity.

 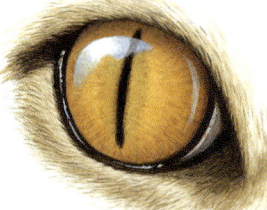

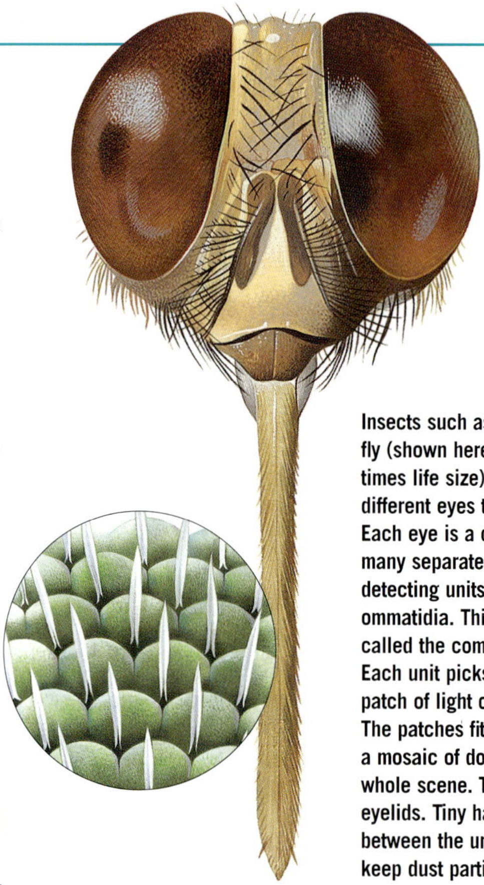

Night Too much bright sunlight would harm a cat's sensitive eyes. The pupil narrows to a slit to stop too much light entering the eye. **Day**

Some animals are nocturnal or active at night. They include cats, mice, bats, owls, and moths. Their large eyes pick up as much of the faint light as possible. Animals that live in total darkness, like moles and cave salamanders or fish at the bottom of the sea, have tiny eyes or none at all.

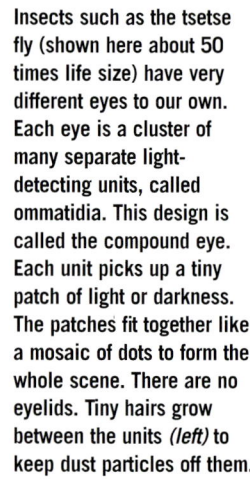

Insects such as the tsetse fly (shown here about 50 times life size) have very different eyes to our own. Each eye is a cluster of many separate light-detecting units, called ommatidia. This design is called the compound eye. Each unit picks up a tiny patch of light or darkness. The patches fit together like a mosaic of dots to form the whole scene. There are no eyelids. Tiny hairs grow between the units *(left)* to keep dust particles off them.

The eye contains specialized nerve endings that detect patterns of light and send information about them to the brain. Other senses work in a similar way. In the ear, the eardrum is a thin piece of skin that vibrates when sounds hit it. Again, nerve endings detect these vibrations. Mammals, birds, lizards, and frogs have eyes and ears on the head. However, some animals have them in other places on the body. A snail has eyes on flexible stalks. A clam has a row of small, simple eyes in the fleshy frill or mantle along the gaping edge of its shell. A grasshopper has eardrums on its knees.

A cat's large eyes see well in the dark, and its large ears pick up faint sounds. The ears can twitch and move to locate the direction of a noise.

ANIMAL BIOLOGY

SMELL AND TASTE

Smell and taste are chemosenses. They are based on the presence of chemical substances, called odorants for smells and flavorants for tastes. We smell airborne odorants with the nose and taste flavorants in food and drink when they touch the tongue. Some animals have chemosensors on other parts of the body, too. A fly can taste with its mouthparts, its antennae (feelers) and its feet. A male moth's feathery antennae can detect special floating chemicals given off by the female moth even if she is one or two miles away.

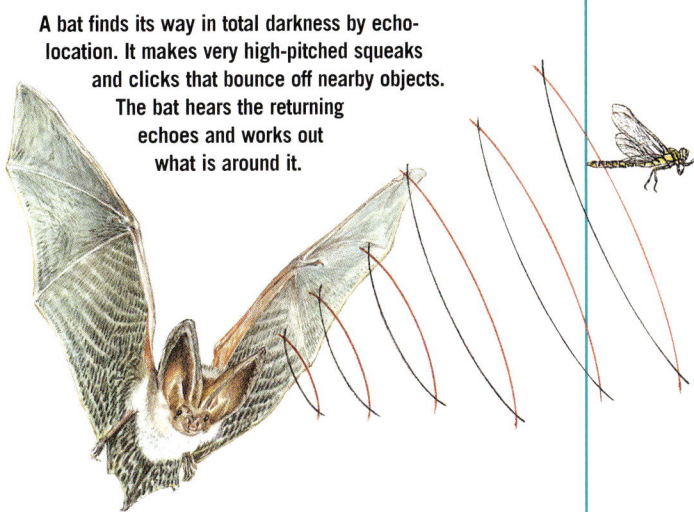

A bat finds its way in total darkness by echo-location. It makes very high-pitched squeaks and clicks that bounce off nearby objects. The bat hears the returning echoes and works out what is around it.

A dog can smell scents up to 10,000 times weaker than we could detect.

For animals in water, smell and taste are much the same. A shark has groups of chemosensors (taste buds) all around the inside of its mouth and also on the front of its snout. They are especially sensitive to blood and body fluids. A catfish has so many chemosensors in the skin all over its body that it is like a "living tongue." Some fish including sharks, rays, and elephant-snout fish (mormyrids) can detect the tiny electrical pulses given off by the active muscles of other animals. They use their electrosense to find prey in cloudy water or hiding in sand and mud.

Electricity travels well in water, so many water animals have evolved to sense it. Electricity does not travel through air so land animals do not sense it. There are other senses that we lack and that we find difficult to imagine. Some animals migrate vast distances across featureless oceans with amazing accuracy *(see page 30)*. They may be able to sense Earth's natural magnetic field or the way our planet's downward pull of gravity varies slightly from place to place.

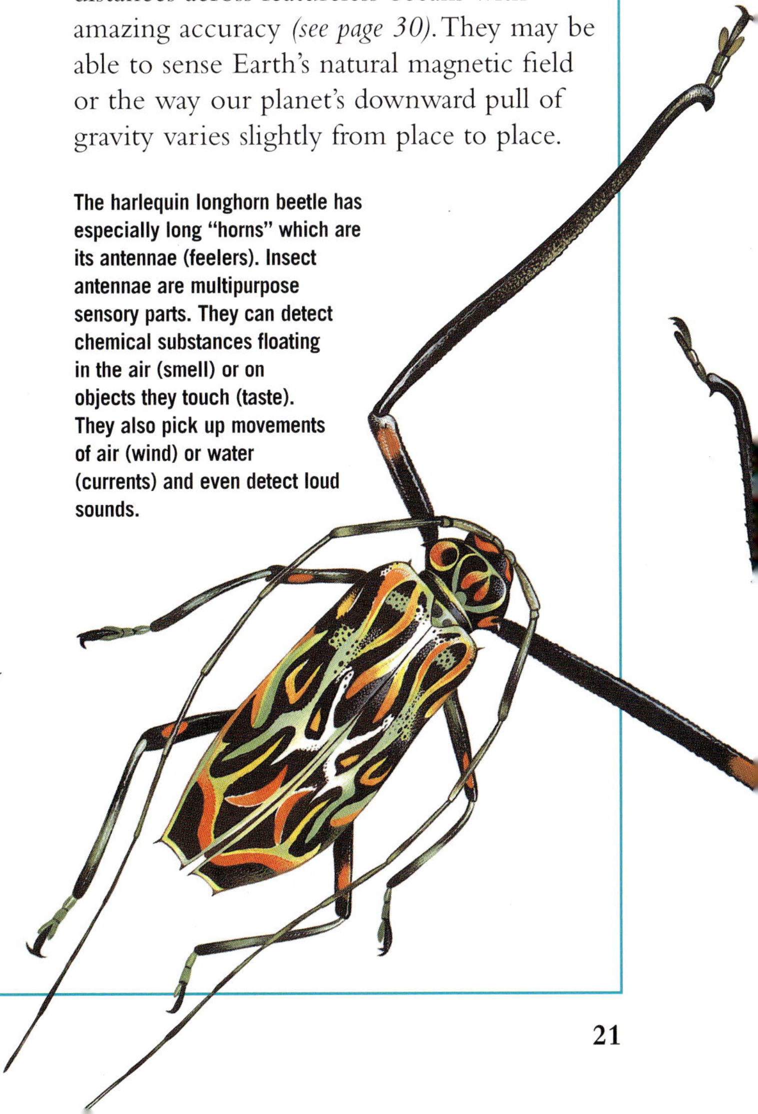

The harlequin longhorn beetle has especially long "horns" which are its antennae (feelers). Insect antennae are multipurpose sensory parts. They can detect chemical substances floating in the air (smell) or on objects they touch (taste). They also pick up movements of air (wind) or water (currents) and even detect loud sounds.

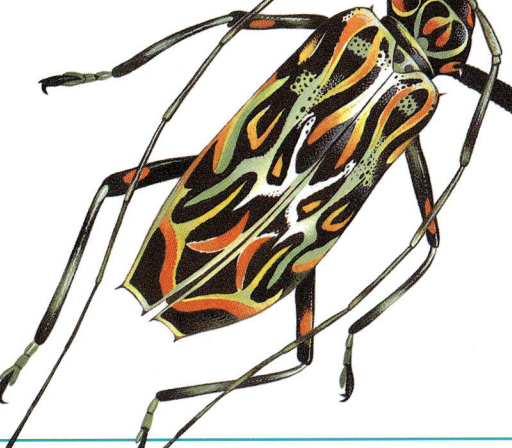

21

ANIMAL BIOLOGY

Movement

ONE OF THE KEY features of an animal is that it moves. It moves parts of its body when it opens its mouth, bends its neck, or curls its tentacles. Most creatures also move about in their surroundings. They run, walk, jump, hop, slither, swim, or fly. A few animals do not move about, at least as adults. Barnacles and mussels are stuck to seashore rocks. But they were mobile during their young, or larval, stages.

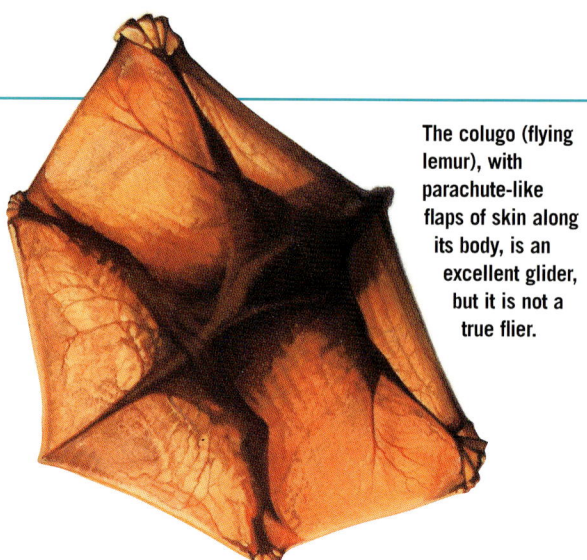

The colugo (flying lemur), with parachute-like flaps of skin along its body, is an excellent glider, but it is not a true flier.

A dolphin moves its tail flukes up and down to provide the forward propulsive force for swimming.

Moving in Air

Only three groups of living animals truly fly in a sustained, controlled way—birds, bats, and insects. Air is so thin it produces little resistance to movement, but it provides very little buoyancy either. Fliers flap their wings down to create a lifting force as well as back to push themselves forward.

Moving in Water

Many animals live in either the sea or in rivers and lakes. Water is much denser than air and so resists movement more. To travel through water quickly, creatures must be smooth and streamlined so the water slips past them easily (submarines are a similar shape for this reason). Fish such as sharks swish their tails from side to side to provide the forward propulsive force for swimming. A fish's fins and a dolphin's flippers provide control for steering, slowing, and going up or down. Penguins flap their wings and "fly" through the water.

A bird holds its feathers flat to form an airtight surface as the wings flap down. Then the feathers swivel to make gaps that allow air through for the upstroke.

The tiger shark (below), a predatory shark, uses its fine sense of smell to detect prey, but relies on its immense speed to carry out its kill. It is one of the fastest sharks, swimming at 25 miles (40 km) per hour.

ANIMAL BIOLOGY

Birds and bats have very thin, light bones to reduce body weight and so save on the energy needed to stay airborne. Even so, they must take in almost twice the amount of energy as food, compared to their ground-dwelling counterparts. The down-flapping wing muscles in the chest are by far the largest muscles in the body of a bird or bat. Insects and bats control their movement by tilting or twisting their wings. Tiny insects like gnats and midges flap their wings nearly 1,000 times each second to stay aloft. Birds control their flight by fanning and twisting their feathers. Hummingbirds are the fastest-flapping birds, with up to 80 wingbeats each minute.

A young orangutan clambers agilely through rain forest trees. It keeps a firm grip on the branches by using its long, flexible fingers and toes.

Beetles have hard wing cases to protect their delicate wings while on the ground. In the air, they spread them open.

All animal movement is made possible by muscles. A gorilla has about 640 muscles, making up about three-fifths of its body weight. A fast fish has 30 to 40 large muscles along each side of its body. Forming nine-tenths of its body weight, they pull on the backbone to swish the tail from side to side.

Moving on Land

Large land animals move in a way suited to their habitat. On open plains, cheetahs, gazelles, and antelopes have long legs and run very fast. Forest animals like deer are slower in straight-line speed, but more agile as they zigzag between trees. Other animals, such as squirrels and sloths, are adapted to moving in the trees themselves. They have long, sharp claws to grip the bark. Central and South American monkeys have long tails, called prehensile tails, that curl around branches like a fifth limb. Limbs are not vital for movement. Many snakes are limbless, yet they can slither on the ground, swim in water, climb trees—and even glide!

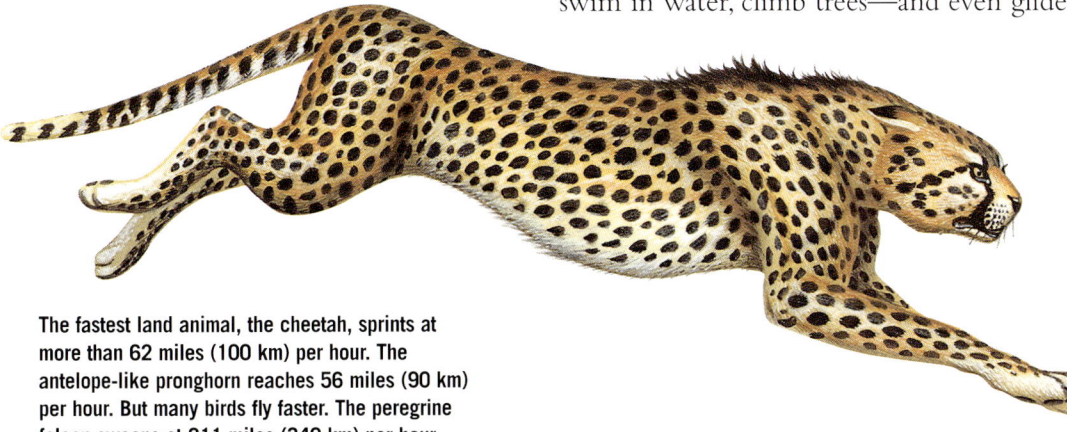

The fastest land animal, the cheetah, sprints at more than 62 miles (100 km) per hour. The antelope-like pronghorn reaches 56 miles (90 km) per hour. But many birds fly faster. The peregrine falcon swoops at 211 miles (340 km) per hour.

ANIMAL SURVIVAL

ADAPTATION

THE PROCESS of evolution (see page 6) ensures that only living things that are suited, or adapted, to their environment will survive. An animal or plant that is poorly adapted to its surroundings soon loses out in the struggle for survival. Animals are adapted to three major features of their environment: the climate (including temperature and rainfall), the food sources available, and avoidance of predators.

The long-eared jerboa has huge back feet to bound over soft desert sand. Its big ears hear well and also give out excess warmth to stop the body overheating.

In hot deserts, smaller animals often hide from the scorching sun by day and come out in the cooler night. They produce very little sweat, urine, or other body liquids, thus saving valuable water.

The camel can go for two weeks without food or water. The body fat in its hump is used as an emergency food store. It can also be broken down by body chemistry to form extra water.

Life thrives in its greatest diversity in warm and moist or wet conditions, such as tropical rain forests and coral reefs. Places that are very cold or very dry provide the greatest challenge to animal survival. Yet some creatures can live in even the driest deserts. They include large animals such as camels and oryx, and smaller creatures like jerboas, lizards, scorpions, and insects.

Protection against predators is vital for smaller animals. The gecko is hunted by birds of prey, snakes, monkeys, small cats, and many other creatures. One of its adaptations is its greenish-brown color and mottled pattern, which help to disguise or camouflage it among branches and leaves. Its strong toes and sharp claws grip the bark well so it can leap away quickly. Also if a predator grabs its tail, this breaks off harmlessly and the gecko can escape.

Desert creatures have adapted in various ways to moving over soft sand. The camel has very wide feet so it does not sink in. Jerboas and gerbils hop and leap on their large back feet. The sidewinder snake moves its body diagonally in a series of Z-shaped stages, pushing sideways against the loose grains. Some desert-dwellers, like the water-holding frog, burrow underground and sleep through the worst of the drought.

24

Only warm-blooded birds and mammals are able to live on land or in the air in the earth's coldest regions, the Arctic and Antarctic ice caps. Reptiles and amphibians would simply be too cold to move. Musk ox, yak, seals, and polar bears have thick furry coats to keep out the chill.

The walrus dives in icy Arctic waters to find its food, mainly shellfish on the sea bed. Under its skin, there is a fatty blubber layer of up to 6 inches (15 cm) thick. The walrus's limbs are adapted as paddles for swimming. Its long tusks act both as levers to pull shellfish off rocks, and as ice picks to haul itself out of the water.

Seashore animals must cope with hot sun, drying winds, crashing waves, frost and snow, heavy rain—and being covered by salt water twice daily at high tide.

Marine polar mammals like walruses and whales have almost no fur at all. But they do have a thick layer of fat under the skin, called blubber, to keep in body warmth. Birds such as penguins also have blubber. Other birds, like the ptarmigan and snowy owl, have extra-thick plumage. They can fluff out their feathers to trap a layer of air that keeps out the cold.

One of the most varied habitats is the coast. The main change here is the twice-daily rise and fall of the tide. Animals such as crabs, worms, shrimp, and shellfish are adapted to being active when they are covered by the seawater—whether it is day or night, winter or summer. Shellfish like limpets have strong outer cases to prevent them drying out at low tide and also being smashed by the waves. Soft-bodied worms and fish burrow in sand or hide under rocks for protection against winds and waves.

One of the most constant habitats is the bottom of the sea. It is always dark and cold, with few water currents. The main problem at great depths is the enormous pressure of the water. Deep-sea fish, starfish and sea cucumbers would go soft and floppy (and die) if brought to the surface.

The polar bear's white fur is camouflage in ice and snow.

The deep-sea cucumber withstands water pressure that would instantly crush a surface animal.

ANIMAL SURVIVAL

ATTACK

MEAT-EATING predators, or carnivores, obtain their food by hunting and attacking other creatures—their prey. Most prey have some form of self-defense *(see opposite)* and so the predator must overcome this. Many predators have strong and agile bodies, quick reactions, keen senses, and hunting weapons such as sharp teeth and long claws. Some use speed to race after their prey. Others lurk hidden among leaves or long grass—perhaps also disguised by camouflage—then ambush their victims *(see pages 18–19)*.

The chameleon's hunting weapon is its sticky-tipped tongue *(above)*. The mantis uses its spiny front legs *(left)*. These hunters sit quite still on a branch, watching and waiting. If an insect comes near, they catch it with lightning speed.

The main hunting weapons of a bird of prey such as the tawny owl are its long sharp claws, called talons. It grabs the prey strongly in these and flies off to its perch. Then it holds the meal down with one foot and uses its hooked beak to tear off pieces small enough to swallow.

Owls use silence and stealth to swoop on prey. The owl's feathers have very soft edges so they make hardly any sound as the bird flaps and glides. The owl can see well at night with its huge eyes. It can hear even better and pinpoint a mouse's footsteps or chewing noises in the darkness.

Many animals use chemical weapons rather than physical ones. Some snakes and spiders have poisonous bites, while wasps and scorpions have venomous stings. The poison can also be used for self-defense as well as subduing prey. These predators usually give warning that they are about to bite or sting an attacker. For example, a rattlesnake shakes its tail, while a poisonous spider rears up to show its fangs. This is because the supply of venom is limited and predators need it to hunt, so they try to avoid using it in defense unnecessarily.

Poisonous snakes bite prey and force venom from their large fangs into the wound. Other snakes are constrictors, like the Indian python. It curls its long body around the victim such as a rat or even a small deer. Each time the prey breathes out the snake tightens its coils until the meal suffocates to death.

ANIMAL SURVIVAL

DEFENSE

PLANT-EATING animals need to defend themselves from carnivores. One defensive strategy is to fight back. Elephants, wild boar, and warthogs can slash with their tusks. Gazelles, antelopes, and wild cattle like musk oxen jab enemies with their sharp horns. Some, like zebras, can kick out powerfully with their hard hooves. Safety in numbers also helps—many eyes and ears are more likely to detect approaching predators. Musk oxen *(below)* form a circle around their young to keep away wolves.

Flying fish leap from the sea's surface and glide on their broad outstretched fins to escape from predators below.

SPINES AND POISONS

One type of physical protection is a hard body case, as in turtles, tortoises, armadillos, snails, and beetles. Another strategy is prickles, spikes, or spines, as in hedgehogs, porcupines, and porcupine fish. Many animals, from mice to deer, rely on their sharp senses, speed, and agility to escape as they dodge or outrun their predators.

The burnet moth is foul-tasting.

The porcupine fish is a spiky ball.

The bush cricket has large eye spots on its wings.

The sea slug has tiny stings on its back.

Certain fish, beetles, caterpillars, moths, and butterflies have horrible-tasting or poisonous flesh. Predators soon learn to avoid them because they advertise this form of defense with bright body patterns called warning colors. Some animals puff up to look bigger, such as puffer fish, toads, and lizards. Another strategy is suddenly to flash bright colors and patterns at the enemy, especially eye spots which resemble or mimic the eyes of an even bigger predator!

ANIMAL SURVIVAL

BEHAVIOR

MANY ANIMALS, from earthworms to whale sharks, lead simple lives. Their behavior is limited and they only encounter others of their kind briefly to mate. Other creatures have much more complex behavior. They form groups, have contests for group supremacy, mates, and territories, help each other when feeding, and even look after each other's offspring.

Living things strive to survive so that they can breed and pass on their genes *(see page 52)* to their offspring. An animal must choose its breeding partner carefully. Courtship behavior and mating displays pick out a partner of the same species, the opposite sex, sexually mature, strong, fit, and healthy. This increases the chances of the offspring being fit and healthy, too.

A pair of albatrosses produces only one chick every two years. So it is important that each parent knows the other is strong and healthy. The two go through a series of actions called a courtship ritual. They extend wings, bob heads, strut about, click beaks, and make various groaning noises. If one partner fails to respond correctly, it may be ill or injured and so less suitable as a parent.

In some animals, survival depends on having a territory. This is a patch of land or water where the owner can live and feed without being in direct competition with rivals of its own kind. Owners often mark their territories by rubbing scents, spraying urine, and leaving piles of droppings around the borders. They defend the territory against other of their kind by calls and songs, and also by visual displays.

In thick forest, visual displays cannot be seen easily. So forest animals use sounds to defend their territories and attract mates. Each morning a howler monkey troop makes its whooping calls. The calls carry for 3 miles (5 km) and are among the loudest sounds in the animal kingdom. Neighboring troops hear the calls and know the territory is occupied. The dawn chorus of birds has the same purpose.

ANIMAL SURVIVAL

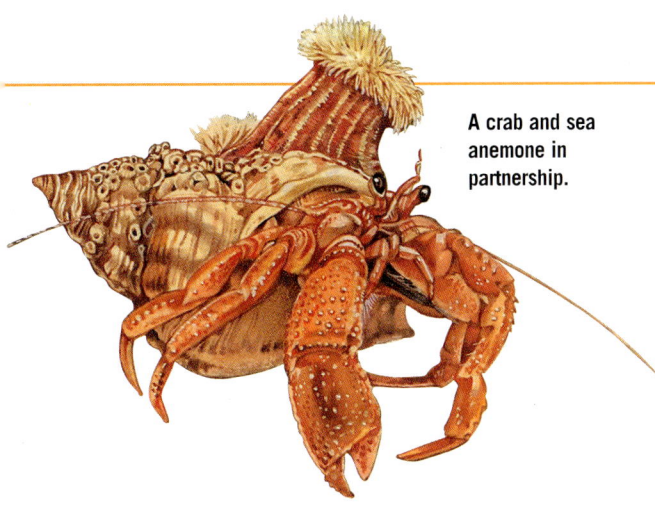

A crab and sea anemone in partnership.

The hermit crab forms a symbiotic partnership with the calliactis sea anemone. The anemone protects the crab with its stinging tentacles. In return the crab carries the anemone to new places to catch victims. Also each partner may share in the leftovers of the other's meal.

HELPING OTHERS

Life in the wild is a battle to stay alive. But sometimes helping others can increase an individual's own chances of survival. Some living things form partnerships with other, quite different species where both partners gain. This is known as symbiosis. Cleaner fish are small fish, such as wrasses, that tend to larger fish. The big fish could easily eat the cleaner. But the cleaner nips fish lice and other pests from its body, mouth, and gills. The big fish is relieved of these parasites and the cleaner fish gets its meal.

Meerkats live in groups of 30 or so. They take turns to be the sentry and watch for predators such as hawks.

Many group-living animals produce alarm calls and actions if they spot danger. This warns others in their group. Likewise if one group member finds a plentiful supply of food, the others gather around to share it. A few kinds of animals even work together to hunt prey. These cooperative killers include wolves, lions, and African wild dogs.

Killer whales, or orcas, live in groups called pods. Members of the pod communicate with each other using sounds, body postures, and actions such as slapping the water with their flippers and tails. They spread out and surround prey such as a shoal of fish or squid. The orcas may then herd the shoal into shallow water or into a cove where they can be caught more easily, one by one. These cooperative hunters also attack seals, sea lions, dolphins, porpoises, and larger whales—even chasing and trapping sea birds on the water's surface.

29

ANIMAL SURVIVAL

MIGRATION

SOME PEOPLE take a vacation each year in warmer parts of the world. Some animals do so, too, although for them it is not for pleasure but for survival. These animals go on migrations—long-distance, usually seasonal, journeys. They stay in an area where there is enough food, water, shelter, or other needs. When conditions change, the animals travel on to find better surroundings, especially a place to breed.

In some cases, the journeys can be fairly random. Herds of wildebeest (gnu) and zebra wander the African plains. They stay in an area while there are plants to eat. Once these are gone, they set off to find an area where recent rains have produced new plant growth. There is usually a yearly pattern to their movements. But sometimes an extra-long dry spell drives them far away.

Monarch butterflies migrate from Canada to Mexico, where they winter clustered together in their thousands on tree trunks *(left)*. They return north in spring, breeding as they go. Some may do a round trip of 4,000 miles.

Another group of migrating birds, such as swallows and swifts, spend spring and summer in northern temperate lands, feeding and breeding. Then, in autumn, they fly south to the warmth of the tropics.

Birds are the main group of migrating animals because their power of flight allows them to cover long distances rapidly. Some land mammals migrate too, such as caribou *(see opposite)*. In Australia, herds of kangaroos and flocks of emus travel hundreds of miles across deserts in search of areas where rain has brought fresh plant growth.

The record migrant, the Arctic tern, flies 15,530 miles (25,000 km) from Antarctica to the Arctic and back each year.

For most migrating creatures the journeys are at a regular time each year and usually follow the same routes as well. In the polar lands of the far north, the summer is short but the long hours of daylight and warmth allow plenty of plant growth. There are few resident animals to eat the plants. So birds such as geese fly up from the south in the spring to feed and raise their young in the Arctic. Then in the autumn, before the long, dark, icy winter grips the polar regions. they return south to temperate Europe, Asia, and North America.

When food is scarce, desert locusts are uncommon. In good conditions they breed well, increase in numbers, band together in vast swarms, and fly off to find new food—often farmers' fields where they devastate the crops.

ANIMAL SURVIVAL

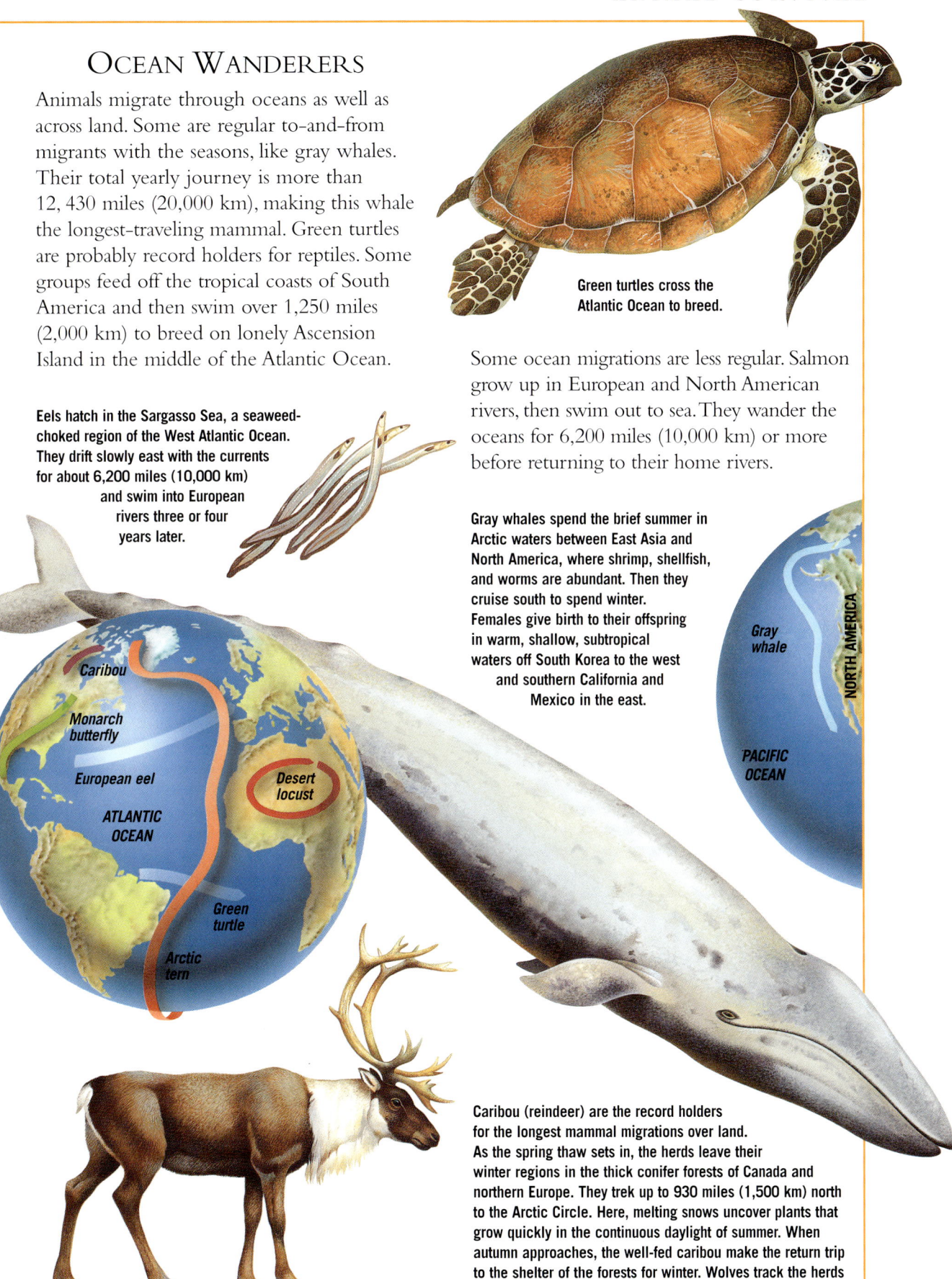

OCEAN WANDERERS

Animals migrate through oceans as well as across land. Some are regular to-and-from migrants with the seasons, like gray whales. Their total yearly journey is more than 12, 430 miles (20,000 km), making this whale the longest-traveling mammal. Green turtles are probably record holders for reptiles. Some groups feed off the tropical coasts of South America and then swim over 1,250 miles (2,000 km) to breed on lonely Ascension Island in the middle of the Atlantic Ocean.

Green turtles cross the Atlantic Ocean to breed.

Eels hatch in the Sargasso Sea, a seaweed-choked region of the West Atlantic Ocean. They drift slowly east with the currents for about 6,200 miles (10,000 km) and swim into European rivers three or four years later.

Some ocean migrations are less regular. Salmon grow up in European and North American rivers, then swim out to sea. They wander the oceans for 6,200 miles (10,000 km) or more before returning to their home rivers.

Gray whales spend the brief summer in Arctic waters between East Asia and North America, where shrimp, shellfish, and worms are abundant. Then they cruise south to spend winter. Females give birth to their offspring in warm, shallow, subtropical waters off South Korea to the west and southern California and Mexico in the east.

Caribou (reindeer) are the record holders for the longest mammal migrations over land. As the spring thaw sets in, the herds leave their winter regions in the thick conifer forests of Canada and northern Europe. They trek up to 930 miles (1,500 km) north to the Arctic Circle. Here, melting snows uncover plants that grow quickly in the continuous daylight of summer. When autumn approaches, the well-fed caribou make the return trip to the shelter of the forests for winter. Wolves track the herds for part of the migration, picking off the stragglers.

HUMAN BODY

HUMAN BODY

THE HUMAN BODY is the most studied object in all of science. Yet every year we learn even more about its most detailed structures and its innermost workings. Even in ancient times people have known basic facts—for example, that there are 206 bones in its skeleton. Since the invention of the microscope nearly 400 years ago, people have studied the body's billions of tiny building blocks, known as cells. In more recent years we have learned about the instructions or "blueprint" for making the body—its genes.

ORGANS AND SYSTEMS

The body's main parts, like the brain, heart, lungs and stomach, are called organs. Different groups of organs work together as systems. Each system has a vital job to keep the whole body alive and healthy. For example, the heart, the body-wide network of tubes, called blood vessels, and the red liquid called blood, together form the circulatory system. This carries essential nutrients and oxygen to all body parts and collects waste materials for disposal. There are about a dozen major systems, shown on the following pages.

KEY
1 Right cerebral hemisphere of brain
2 Left cerebral hemisphere of brain
3 Pituitary gland
4 Nose cartilage
5 Tear gland
6 Eyelid muscle
7 Eye orbit (socket)
8 Inner ear
9 Eardrum
10 Outer ear canal
11 Outer ear

KEY continued
36 Liver
37 Gall bladder
38 Right adrenal gland
39 Right kidney
40 Pancreas
41 Left adrenal gland
42 Left kidney
43 Stomach
44 Spleen
45 Small intestine
46 Large intestine
47 Appendix
48 Right ureter
49 Left ureter
50 Bladder

32

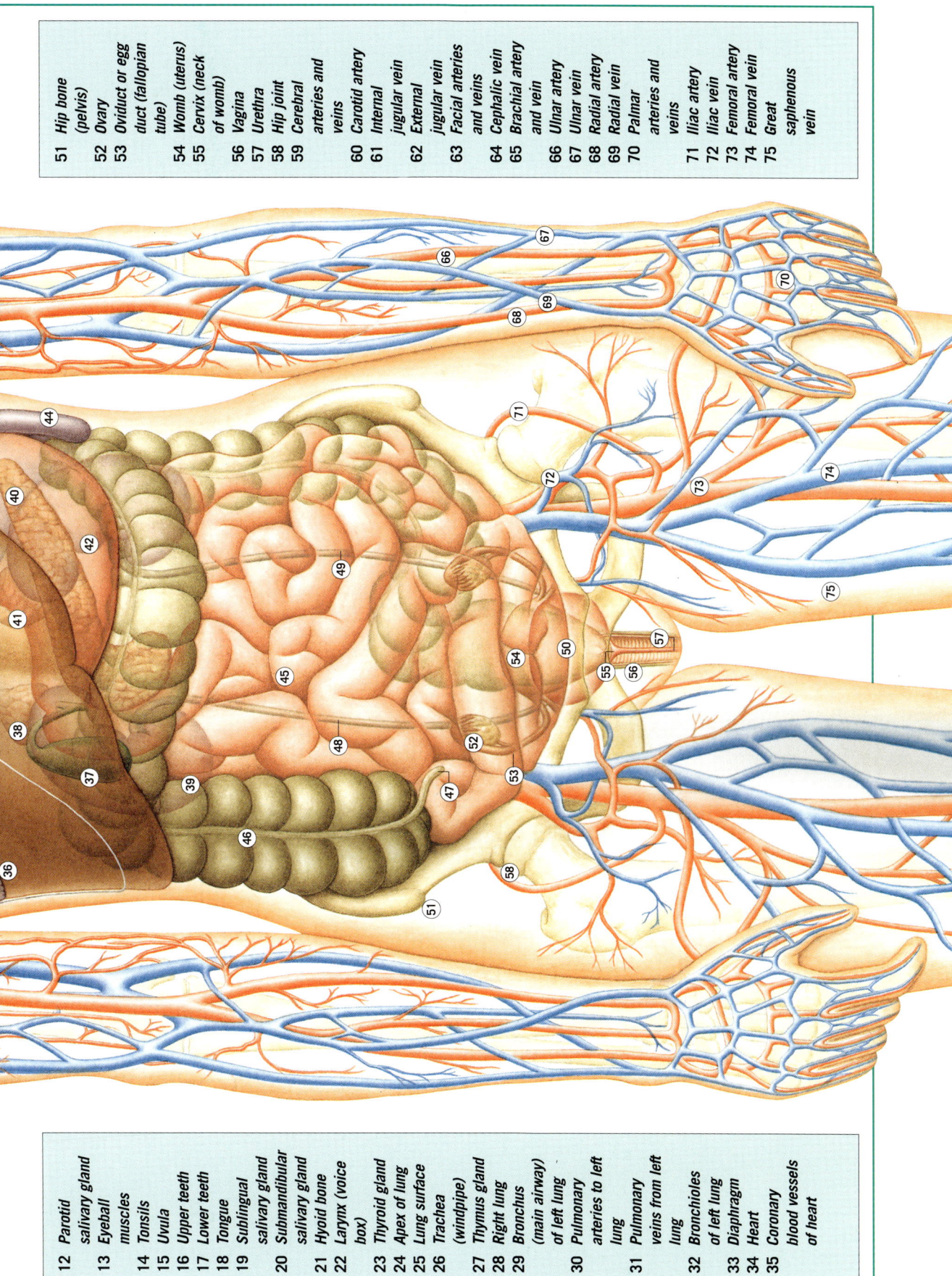

HUMAN BODY

DIGESTION 1

THE BODY NEEDS energy to power its chemical life processes. It also needs raw materials for maintenance, growth, and repair. The energy and raw materials are in our food. Digestion is the process of taking in, or eating, food and breaking it down into tiny pieces, small enough to pass into the blood and be carried all around the body. The parts that take in and break down food are known as the digestive system.

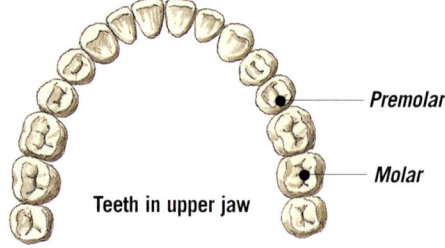
Teeth in upper jaw — Premolar, Molar

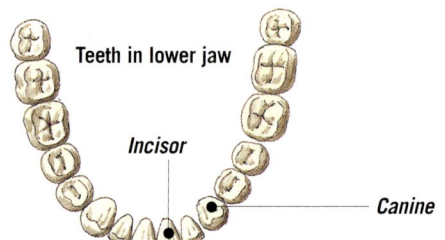
Teeth in lower jaw — Incisor, Canine

An adult person has 32 teeth. There are four incisors at the front of each jaw. Behind these on each side are one canine, two premolars and three molars.

TEETH

There are four main kinds of teeth. The sharp-edged, chisel-like incisors at the front of the mouth slice and cut pieces from large food items. The taller, pointed canines tear and rip tough food. The premolars and molars at the back of the mouth squeeze and crush the food. Each tooth has a long root that fixes it firmly in the jaw bone, and a crown that sticks up above the soft, pink gum. The whitish enamel covering the crown is the hardest substance in the body.

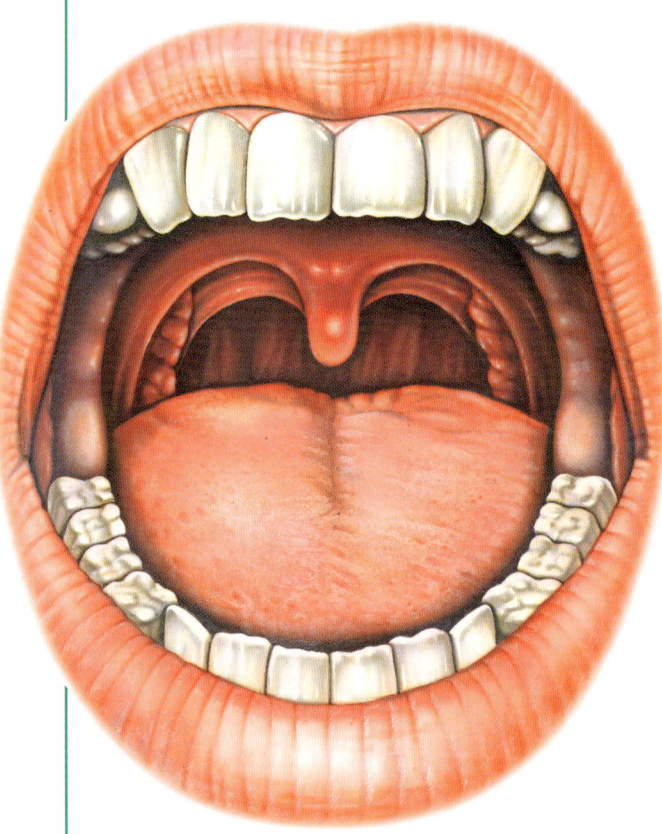

The mouth is the entrance to the digestive system. Here, food is chewed and moistened.

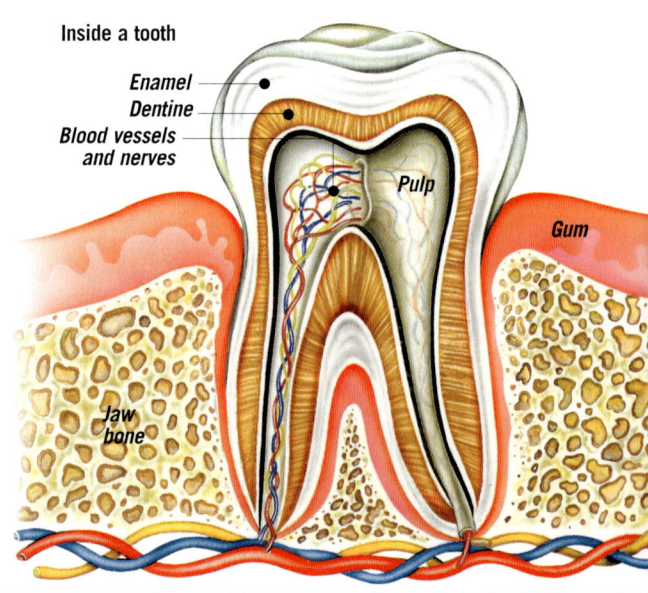

Inside a tooth — Enamel, Dentine, Blood vessels and nerves, Pulp, Gum, Jaw bone

INSIDE THE MOUTH

The teeth cut off and chew pieces of food into a soft pulp. Saliva (spit) makes the food moist and slippery, for easy swallowing. The tongue tastes the food, to make sure it is not bad or rotten, and moves it around in the mouth, for thorough chewing. The lips seal at the front of the mouth to stop food and drink from dribbling out during chewing.

HUMAN BODY

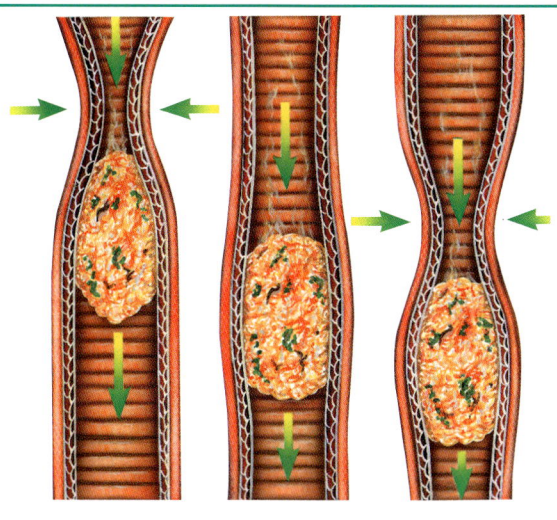

Food is pushed down the esophagus and through the stomach and intestines by waves of muscular squeezing (peristalsis).

Two large organs aid the process of digestion. The pancreas gland is wedge-shaped and lies behind the stomach on the left. It makes strong digestive juices that flow along a tube, the pancreatic duct, into the small intestine. These juices dissolve the food further. The other organ is the liver *(see page 36)*, in front of the stomach on the right. It makes a yellow-green liquid, bile. This is stored in the gall bladder and then added to the food in the small intestine, to help digest fatty foods.

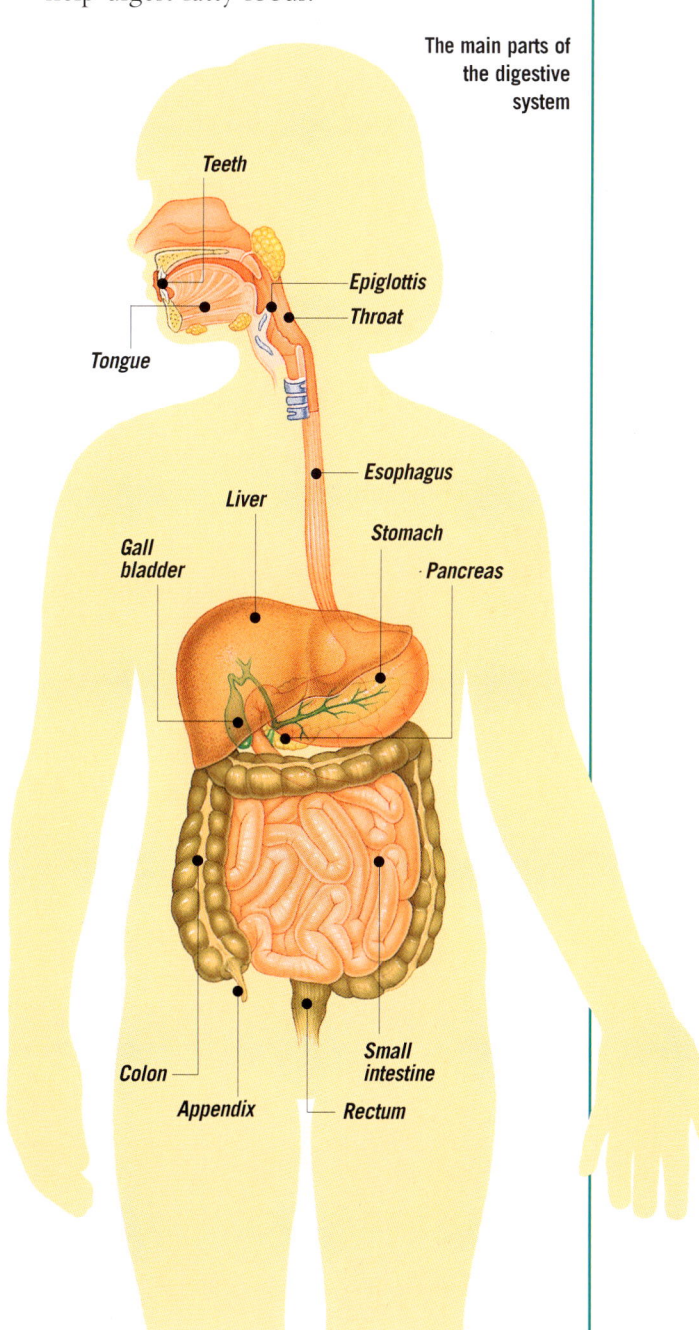

ESOPHAGUS AND STOMACH

Swallowed food is squeezed down the esophagus by wavelike muscular contractions of its wall, called peristalsis. The food enters the stomach, a J-shaped muscular bag. This expands like a balloon to hold about three quarts of food and drink. It churns up the food, mixing in its strong digestive juices to break it into smaller and smaller particles. An average meal takes between three and six hours to be digested in the stomach. If the food is bad or unsuitable in some way, peristalsis works in reverse and pushes it up and out of the mouth, a process called vomiting.

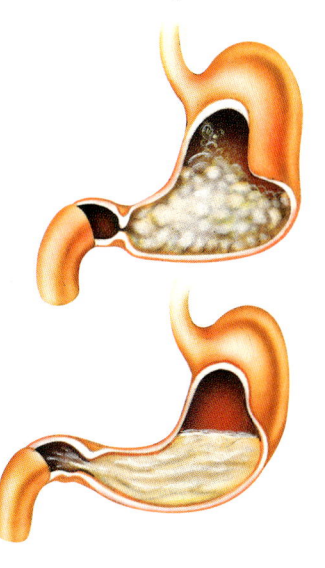

The stomach stretches as it fills with food, then digests the food by physical and chemical processes. The muscular walls of the stomach writhe and squirm to squash and pulverize the food physically. Also, the lining of the stomach makes powerful digestive juices, including acids and enzymes. These pour onto the food and mix with it, to dissolve it chemically. The result is a creamy soup called chyme. This oozes slowly into the next part of the digestive system, the small intestine.

The main parts of the digestive system

- Teeth
- Tongue
- Epiglottis
- Throat
- Esophagus
- Liver
- Stomach
- Gall bladder
- Pancreas
- Colon
- Appendix
- Small intestine
- Rectum

35

HUMAN BODY

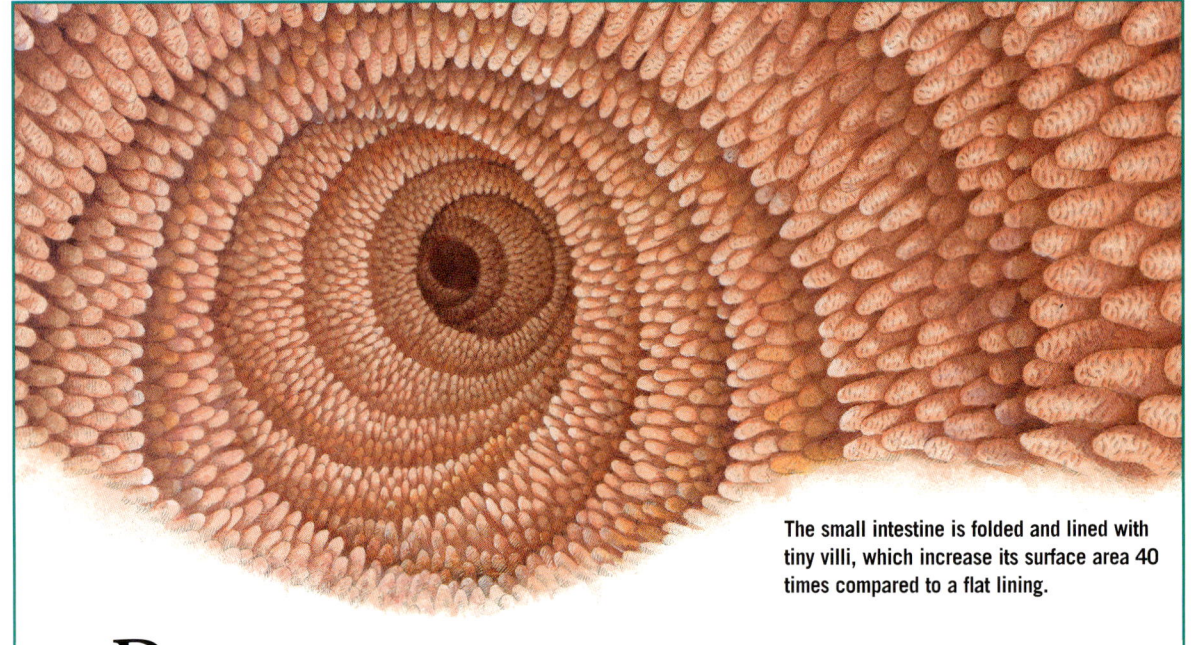

The small intestine is folded and lined with tiny villi, which increase its surface area 40 times compared to a flat lining.

DIGESTION II

THE ENTIRE digestive system, from the mouth to the anus, is about 30 feet (9.1 m) long. Looped and coiled into the lower abdomen *(see page 35),* the small intestine makes up two-thirds of this length. Digestive juices from the small intestine's lining are added to the food to complete its chemical breakdown. The resulting nutrients are so small that they can pass through the lining into the blood, to be carried away to the liver. The liver acts as a kind of food processor, making new chemicals from the nutrients it receives and storing them until they are required. Those substances the body does not need, including impurities in the blood, it sends on to the kidneys.

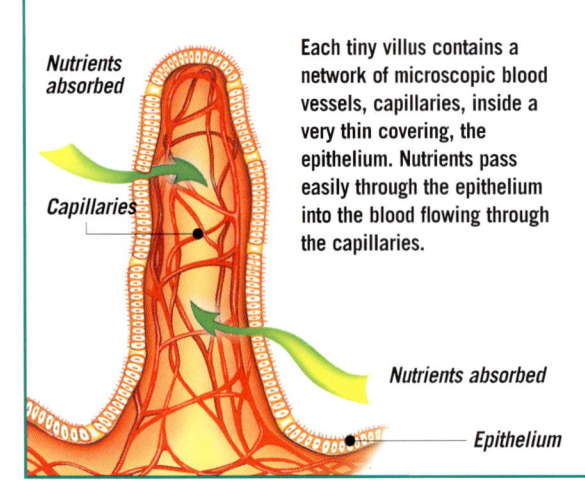

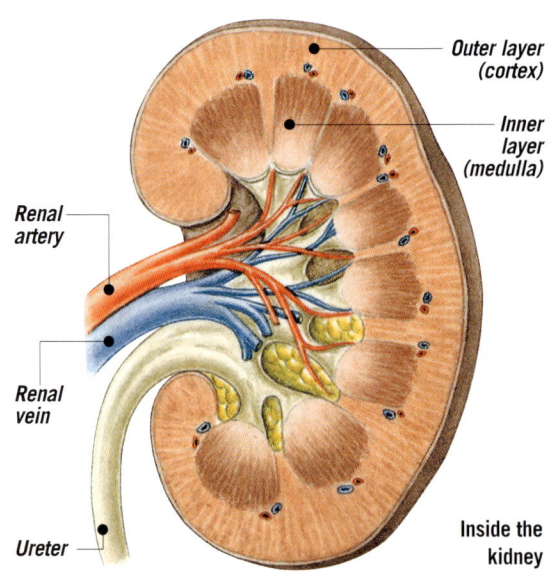

Each tiny villus contains a network of microscopic blood vessels, capillaries, inside a very thin covering, the epithelium. Nutrients pass easily through the epithelium into the blood flowing through the capillaries.

Inside the kidney

THE KIDNEYS

The two kidneys receive a very large flow of blood—more than one quart per minute. It passes through about one million microscopic filtering units, called nephrons, packed into the outer layer of each kidney. The nephrons remove waste substances and excess water from the blood. These flow through the kidney's inner layer, where some water is taken back into the blood according to the body's needs. The resulting liquid waste is called urine. It dribbles down a tube, the ureter, to a stretchy bag in the lower abdomen, the bladder. It is stored here until it can be passed to the outside.

HUMAN BODY

NUTRIENTS

THE BODY NEEDS a wide range of nutrients to stay healthy. There are six main groups of nutrients—proteins, fats, carbohydrates, vitamins, minerals, and fiber. Different kinds of foods are rich in different groups *(see illustration below)*. Proteins are found in meat, poultry, fish, milk, beans, and green vegetables. They help to build and maintain muscles and other body parts, so they are important for growth. Fats (lipids)

VITAMINS AND MINERALS

Many vitamins and minerals are needed for good health, but usually in small amounts. Vitamins have letters such as A, B, and C. Lack of a vitamin may cause illness. For example, lack of vitamin A from tomatoes, carrots, cheese, fish, and liver may result in poor eyesight. Minerals include calcium and iron. Iron is found in meat, green vegetables, and nuts. It is needed for healthy blood. Its lack causes a type of anemia.

Fats (lipids)

Fiber

Iron (a mineral)

Carbohydrates

Vitamin A

Proteins

are found in meat, dairy products, and some oily fruits and vegetables like avocado, olives, and sunflower seeds. Small amounts are needed to build the walls around the body's microscopic cells, and also for healthy nerves. Carbohydrates such as starches and sugars are found in bread, pasta, rice and other grains, and potatoes. They are the main source of energy for movement, digestion, and other life processes.

FIBER

Fiber is found only in plant foods, chiefly in breads, pastas, and other products made from whole grains or cereals, and also in many fresh fruits and vegetables. Fiber is not actually digested and absorbed by the body, but it helps the digestive system to work effectively and stay healthy. It adds bulk to the food so that the stomach and intestines can grip and squeeze the food along.

HUMAN BODY

BREATHING

THE BODY needs continual supplies of oxygen. This invisible gas makes up about one-fifth of the air around us. It is needed for chemical processes inside the body's cells *(see page 52)* that release energy from food. Breathing draws air into the body so that oxygen can be absorbed.

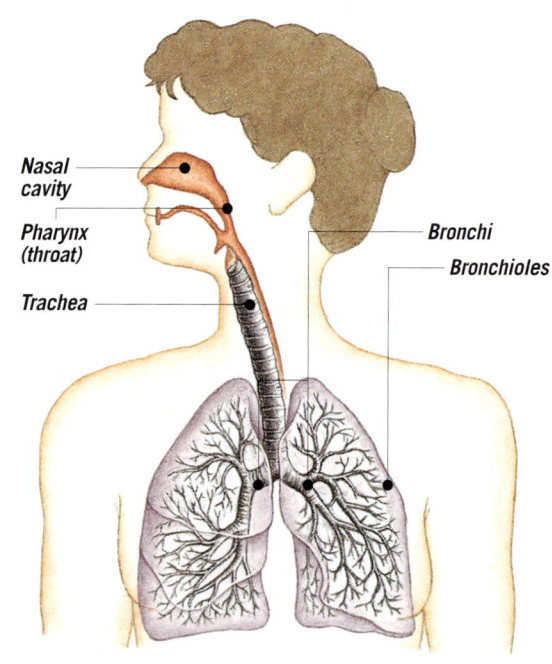

The two lungs almost fill the chest. Air passes into them along the trachea. This divides at its base into two tubes, the primary bronchi, one to each lung.

- Nasal cavity
- Pharynx (throat)
- Trachea
- Bronchi
- Bronchioles

- Terminal bronchiole
- Arteriole (tiny artery)
- Venule (tiny vein)
- Alveoli
- High-oxygen blood (red)
- Low-oxygen blood (blue)

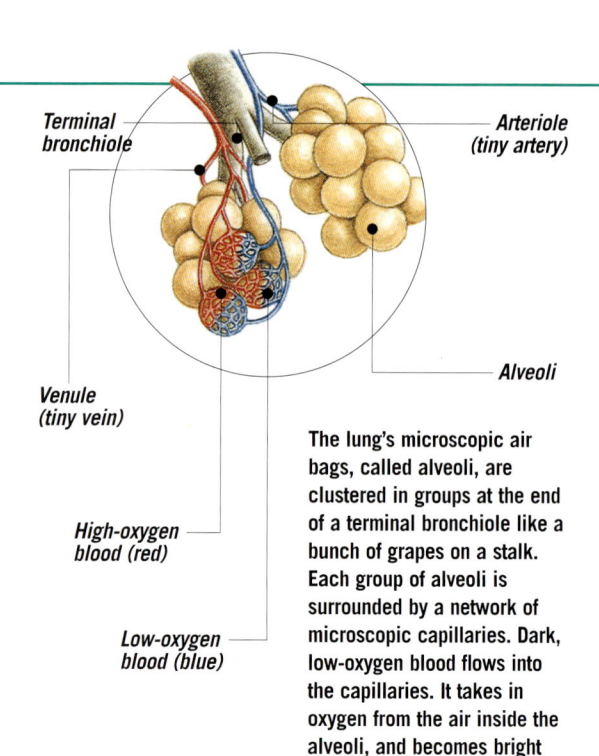

The lung's microscopic air bags, called alveoli, are clustered in groups at the end of a terminal bronchiole like a bunch of grapes on a stalk. Each group of alveoli is surrounded by a network of microscopic capillaries. Dark, low-oxygen blood flows into the capillaries. It takes in oxygen from the air inside the alveoli, and becomes bright red, high-oxygen blood.

Each terminal bronchiole ends in a cluster of microscopic air bubbles, called alveoli. There are about 300 million alveoli in each lung, giving the whole lung a spongy texture. Besides fresh air, the lungs also receive low-oxygen blood from the heart along the pulmonary arteries. These divide and form networks of microscopic blood vessels (capillaries) around the alveoli. Oxygen from the air inside the alveoli passes easily through the thin walls of the alveoli and capillaries into the blood. This high-oxygen blood returns along pulmonary veins to the heart.

RESPIRATORY SYSTEM

The respiratory system draws fresh air into the body, absorbs the vital oxygen from it into the blood, and then passes the stale air out again. The main parts of the system where oxygen is absorbed are the lungs. Breathing muscles stretch the lungs to make them larger and suck in air. These muscles are the diaphragm below the lungs, and the intercostal muscles between the ribs *(right)*. Fresh air passes in through the nose and mouth, down the pharynx (throat) and trachea (windpipe), into the lungs. The lung airways, called bronchi, divide many times and become thinner, ending in terminal bronchioles, narrower than human hairs.

Breathing in—diaphragm flattens, ribs tilt up and out.

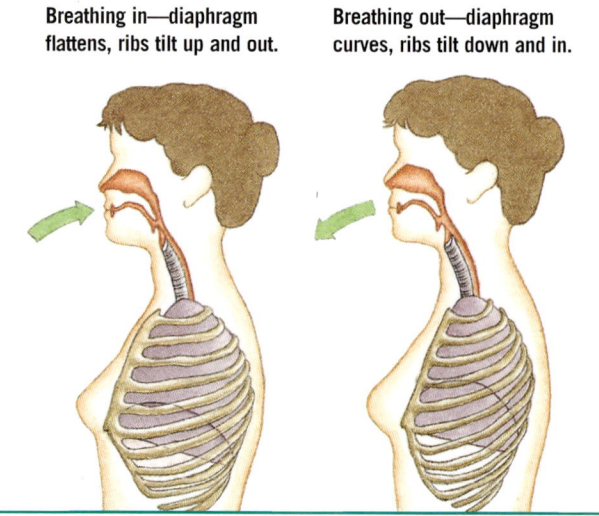

Breathing out—diaphragm curves, ribs tilt down and in.

HUMAN BODY

BREATHING RATE

As oxygen passes from the air in the alveoli into the blood, the waste substance carbon dioxide passes the opposite way, from the blood into the air. This stale air is then pushed out of the lungs when the breathing muscles relax and the stretched lungs spring back to their smaller size. At rest, an adult person breathes in and out about 12 times each minute. Each breath is around one pint of air. After running a race, a person may breathe 60 times each minute and take in more than two quarts of air each time, to obtain extra oxygen for the active muscles.

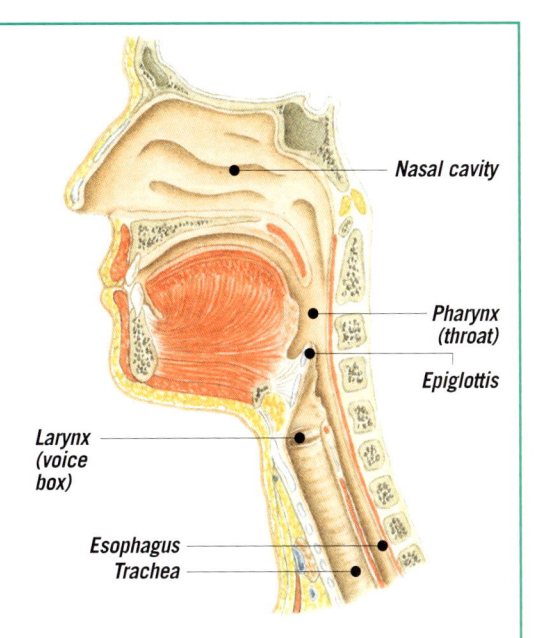

The voice box is at the top of the trachea, where it joins the lower throat. It is a box shape made of plates of cartilage (gristle).

Unlike fish, people cannot breathe under water. Scuba divers carry their own air supply. The air in the tanks is compressed so that a lot fits into a small space.

CLEANING THE LUNGS

The lungs are delicate and easily damaged. Hairs in the nose filter bits of floating dust and other particles from air as it is breathed in. The airways are lined by sticky mucus which traps dirt and dust. Microscopic hairs, called cilia, line the smaller airways. They sweep mucus and trapped dirt into the throat, where it can be swallowed.

SPEECH

Air emerging from the lungs not only carries waste carbon dioxide. It has another use—speech. At the top of the trachea is the larynx (voice box). This has a shelflike fold of cartilage projecting from each side, known as the vocal cords. To speak, muscles pull the vocal cords together so that there is only a very narrow slit between them. Air rushing through the slit makes the cords shake or vibrate, which produces sounds. These sounds are shaped into clear words by movements of the mouth, cheeks, teeth, tongue, and lips.

Muscles stretch the vocal cords longer and tighter to make higher-pitched sounds.

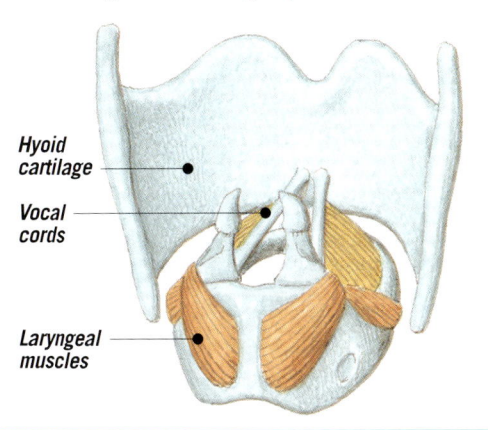

39

HEART

ALL THE MUSCLES and tissues that make up the body must be continually supplied with food and oxygen. This job is carried out by the blood circulatory system.

The heart lies at the center of the circulatory system and pumps the blood around the body. About the size of your fist, it is an incredibly strong organ, made entirely of muscle. It beats more than two billion times during the average life span of a person and pumps about 340 quarts of blood every hour—enough to fill a car's gasoline tank every seven minutes.

Blood containing fresh oxygen travels from the lungs to the heart through the pulmonary veins. At the same time, blood with very little oxygen left in it returns to the heart along veins from the muscles and tissues. The heart pumps the fresh blood to the rest of the body and the exhausted blood to the lungs. It pumps the blood at high pressure so that it can travel upward to the head—against gravity—as well as downward. You can feel this pumping action by placing your fingers on the inside of your wrist or the side of your neck, both points where a main artery lies close to the surface of your skin.

The heart has four chambers (left and right atria, left and right ventricles). Flaps, called valves, slam shut to prevent blood leaking back once it has entered each chamber (this is the heartbeat you can hear in someone's chest). Blood arrives in the heart through the pulmonary veins from the lungs *(shown in red in the diagrams below)*, and through the vena cava from the rest of the body *(shown in blue)*. The heart then squeezes inward and the blood is pushed out. Some travels along the pulmonary arteries to the lungs; the rest passes through the aorta to the body.

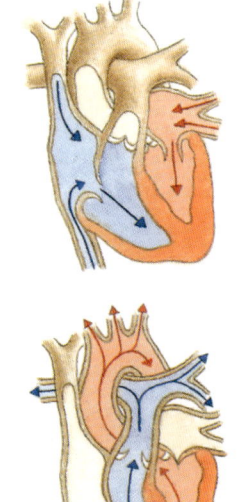

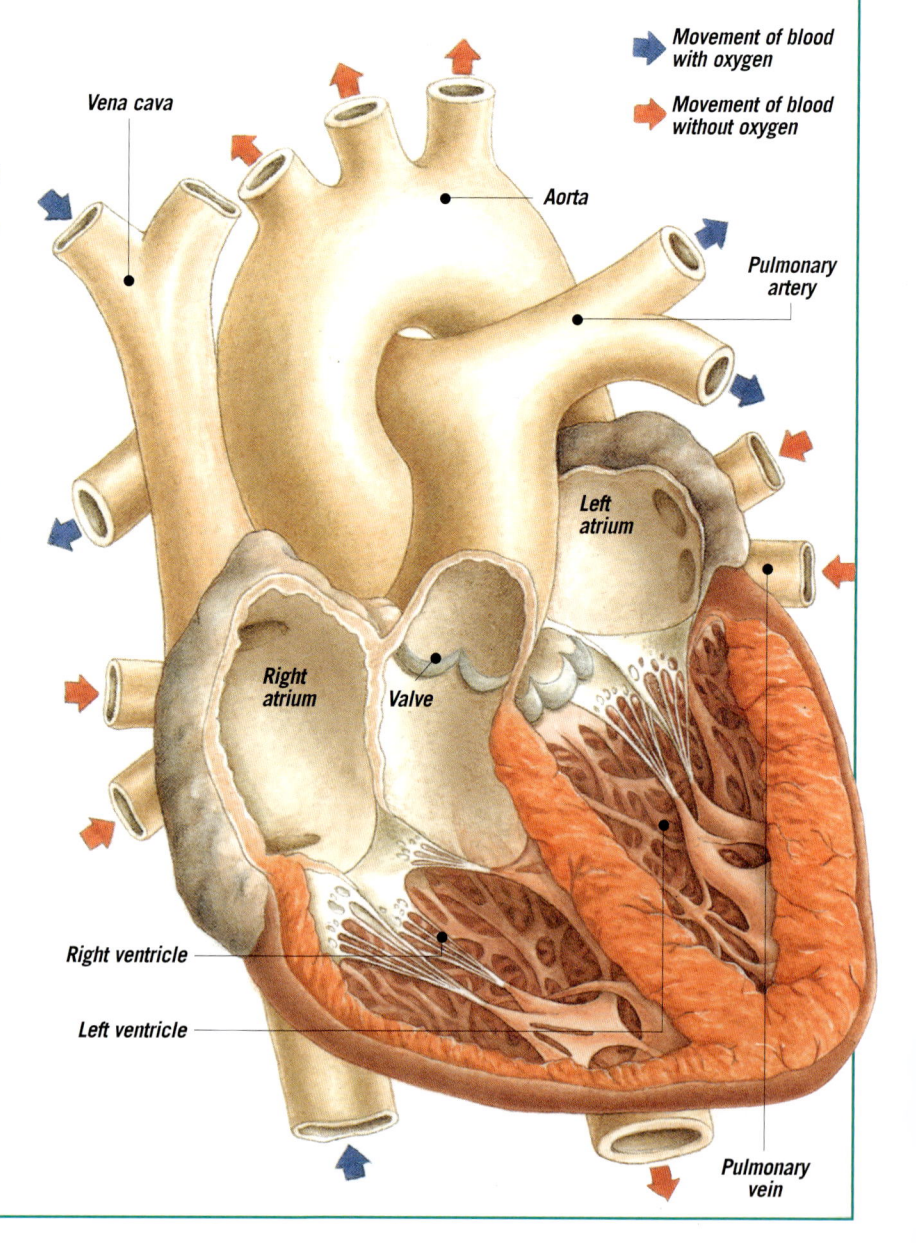

Movement of blood with oxygen

Movement of blood without oxygen

Vena cava

Aorta

Pulmonary artery

Left atrium

Right atrium

Valve

Right ventricle

Left ventricle

Pulmonary vein

HUMAN BODY

BLOOD

PUMPED by the heart, blood collects oxygen from the lungs and dissolved food from the liver and delivers it to all parts of the body. It also clears away waste, helps cool the body when it overheats, clots when the skin is damaged and protects against invading bacteria and viruses.

The veins and arteries in your body look like a page in a road atlas. There are highways, the main blood-carrying tubes or vessels, which lead out from the heart to the limbs and the head. There are also lanes and tracks, tiny vessels called capillaries that reach all the cells in the body.

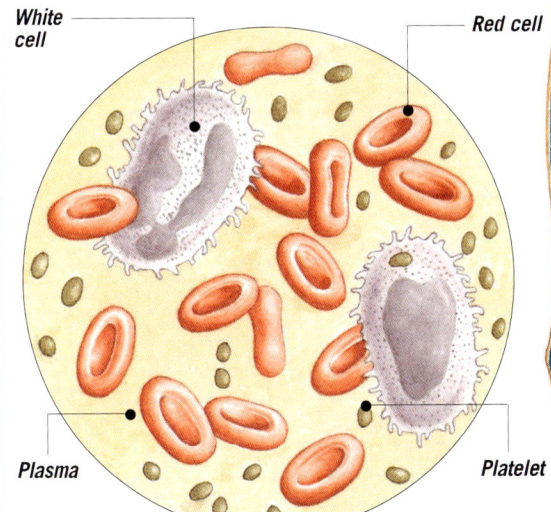

White cell — *Red cell* — *Plasma* — *Platelet*

Seen under a very powerful microscope, blood is made up of a number of cells. A drop of blood the size of a pinhead would contain about 5 million red cells.

Blood is made up of millions of tiny cells floating in a yellowish, watery fluid called plasma. There are red cells, used for carrying oxygen, white cells, which fight any infection by invading bacteria or viruses, and platelets, which make the blood clot when a vessel is damaged, so sealing the wound. Different kinds of white cell work together to protect you from disease: T-cells, which identify invaders; B-cells, which make deadly proteins called antibodies that surround the invaders; and macrophages, which swallow them up and destroy them.

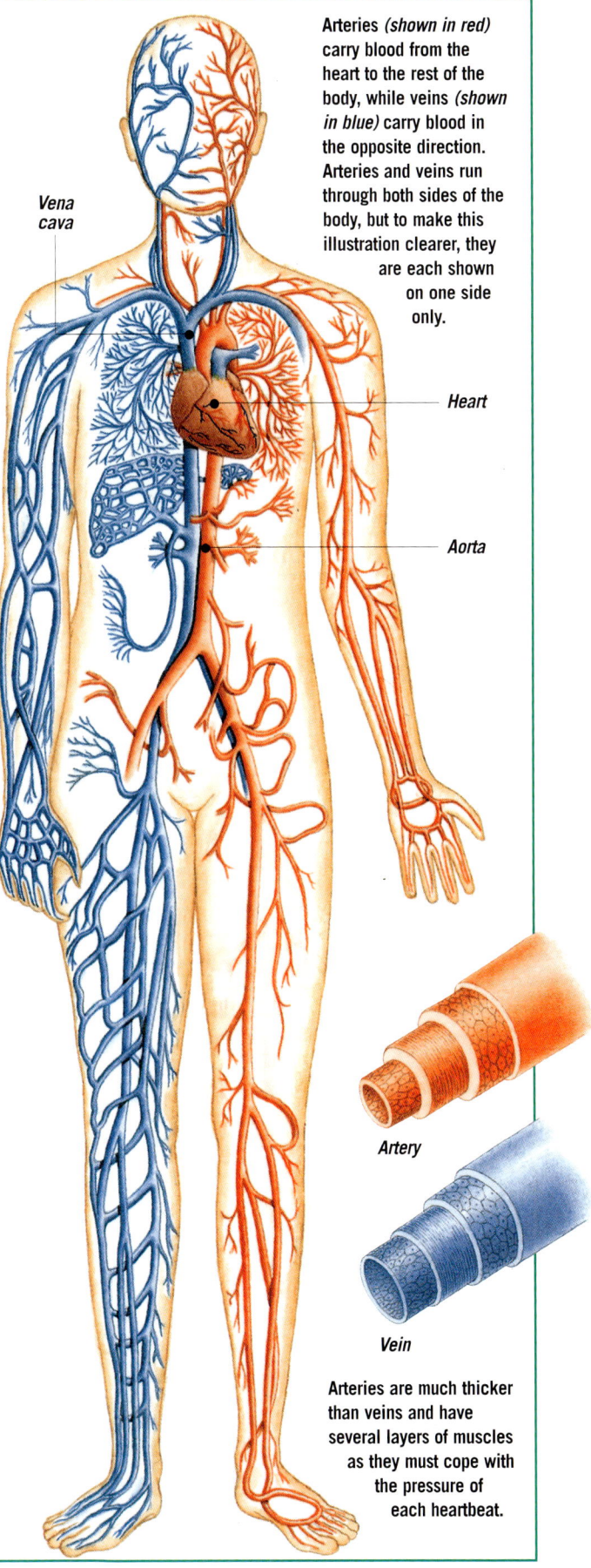

Vena cava — *Heart* — *Aorta*

Arteries *(shown in red)* carry blood from the heart to the rest of the body, while veins *(shown in blue)* carry blood in the opposite direction. Arteries and veins run through both sides of the body, but to make this illustration clearer, they are each shown on one side only.

Artery — *Vein*

Arteries are much thicker than veins and have several layers of muscles as they must cope with the pressure of each heartbeat.

41

HUMAN BODY

SKELETON

THE 206 BONES of the skeleton form a strong inner framework for the rest of the body, which is soft and floppy. Different parts of the skeleton work in different ways. The skull is a domed protective case for the brain. The backbones, or vertebrae, are a strong yet flexible central support. The long bones of the limbs work like levers.

SKELETON KEY
A Cranium (skull)
B Mandible (lower jaw)
C Sternum (breastbone)
D Ribs
E Clavicle (collar bone)
F Scapula (shoulder blade)
G Humerus
H Radius
J Ulna
K Carpals (wrist bones)
L Metacarpals
M Phalanges of fingers
N Sacrum
P Coccyx
Q Pelvis (hip bone)
R Femur
S Patella (knee cap)
T Fibula
U Tibia
V Tarsals (ankle bones)
W Metatarsals
X Phalanges of toes

MUSCLES

ABOUT TWO-FIFTHS of the body's weight is made up by its muscles—some 640 of them. Most are attached to the bones of the skeleton and pull on them to make the body move. In each part of the body the muscles are in two main layers. There are superficial muscles just under the skin and deep muscles lying below them next to the bones.

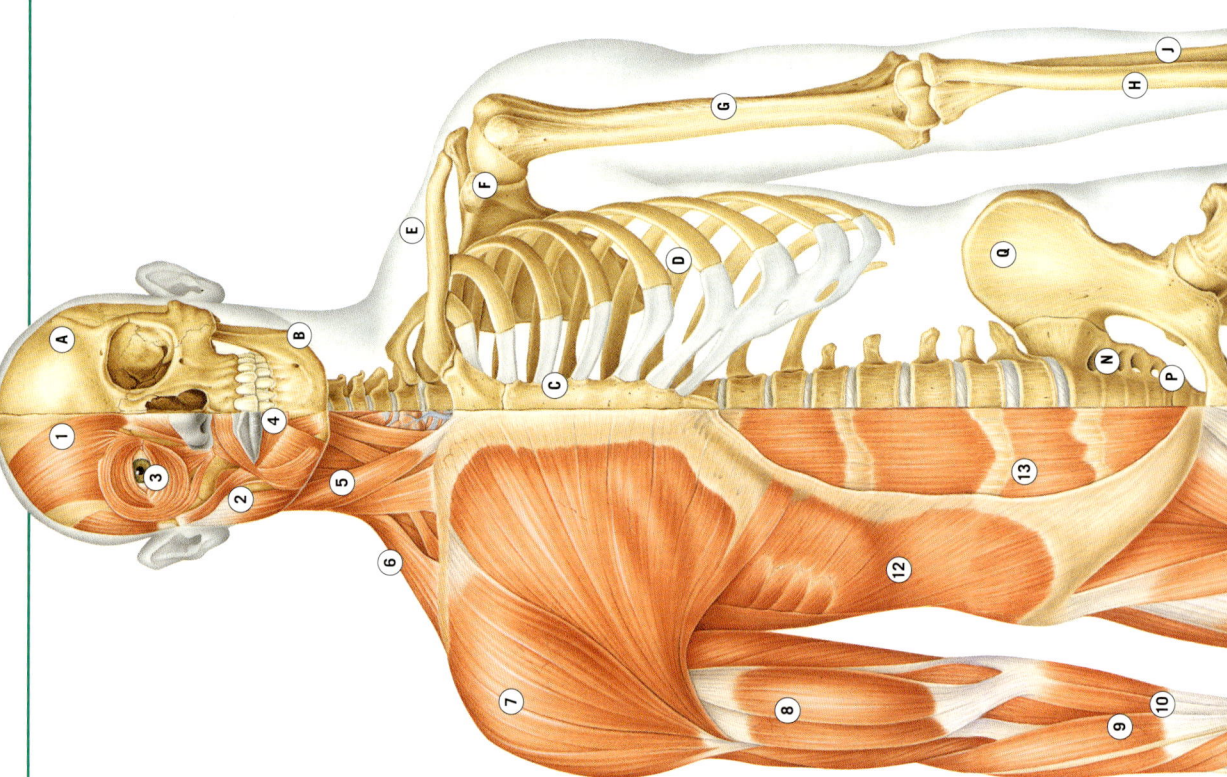

MUSCLE KEY
1 Frontalis
2 Masseter
3 Orbicularis oculi
4 Orbicularis oris
5 Sternocleidomastoid
6 Trapezius
7 Deltoid
8 Biceps brachii
9 Brachioradialis
10 Finger flexors
11 Carpal sheath
12 External oblique
13 Rectus abdominis
14 Sartorius
15 Rectus femoris
16 Vastus lateralis
17 Vastus medialis
18 Tibialis anterior
19 Gastrocnemius
20 Peroneus longus
21 Toe extensors
22 Tarsal sheath

42

HUMAN BODY

Cranium (skull)
5 cervical vertebrae
Scapula
12 thoracic vertebrae
12 pairs of ribs
5 lumbar vertebrae
Sacrum
Ischium of pelvis
Pubis of pelvis
Calcaneus

Trapezius
Deltoid
Triceps
Latissimus dorsi
Finger flexors
Finger extensors
Gluteus maximus
Semitendinosus
Gastrocnemius
Soleus
Peroneus

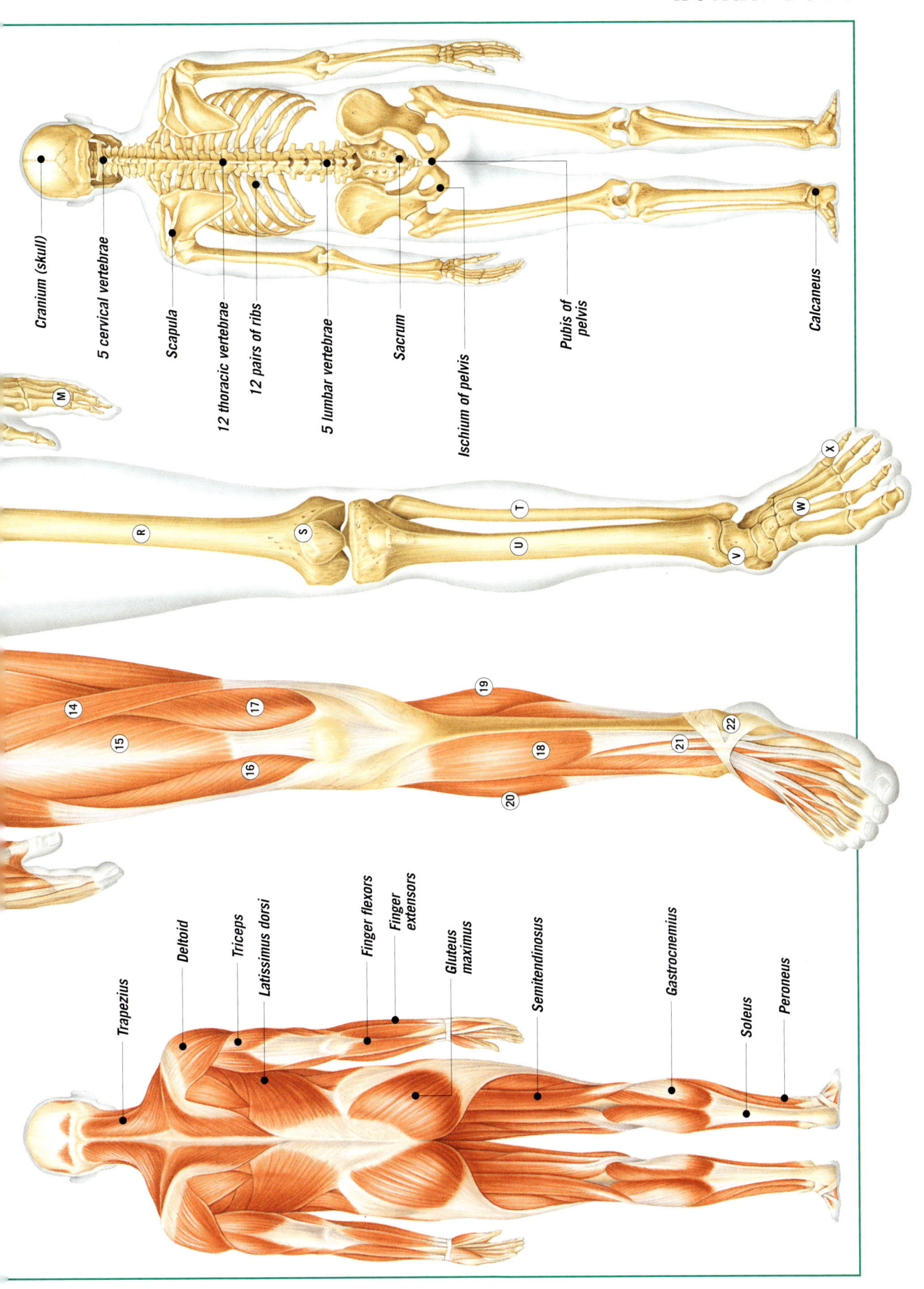

43

HUMAN BODY

MUSCLES

EVERY MOVEMENT that the body makes is powered by muscles. A muscle is a body part designed to get shorter or contract *(see page 42)*. Most muscles are long and slim. They taper at each end into a ropelike tendon which is attached firmly to a bone of the skeleton. As the muscle contracts, it becomes thicker and pulls on the bone, moving that part of the body.

The largest muscle is the gluteus maximus in the buttock. It pulls the thigh bone backward at the hip when you walk, and with greater speed and power when you run and jump. The smallest muscle is the stapedius, deep inside the ear. It is just a few hundredths of an inch long and thinner than cotton thread. It pulls on a tiny ear bone, the stirrup, to prevent very loud noises from damaging the delicate inner ear.

Biceps shortens

A muscle can only pull on a bone, not push it. So most muscles have opposing partners, like the biceps and triceps in the upper arm. The biceps shortens and pulls the lower arm to bend the elbow. The triceps shortens and pulls to straighten the elbow, as the biceps relaxes.

A muscle contains many bundles of fibers. In turn, each fiber is made of even thinner fibrils.

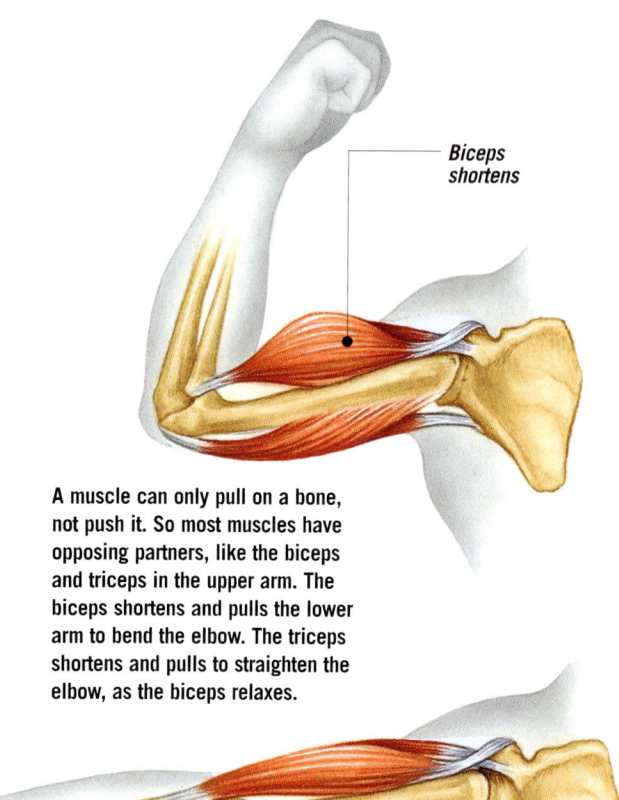

Actin and myosin in fibril
Muscle fibril
Muscle fiber
Bundles of muscle fibers
Cross section of a muscle
Triceps shortens

HOW MUSCLES WORK

Each muscle is linked by nerves to the brain. The muscle itself is made up of bundles of hair-thin muscle fibers, which contain even thinner microscopic fibrils. In turn, each muscle fibril contains bundles of long, chainlike substances. These are muscle proteins, called actin and myosin.

When you want to contract a muscle, the brain sends signals along the nerve to the muscle. The signals make the actin and myosin proteins slide past each other, rather like people pulling hand-over-hand on a rope. Each protein slides together only a hundredth of an inch. But these tiny movements build up in the thousands of fibrils contained inside the hundreds of fibers. Most muscles can shorten to about two-thirds of their relaxed length.

Sheath around whole muscle

HUMAN BODY

Muscles in Action

Blinking your eye involves the movement of just one muscle, called the orbicularis oculi, an O-shaped muscle inside the eyelid. It is attached not to bones, but to other muscles and soft tissues. When it shortens, the two sides of the O move together and close the gap between them. The lip muscle, the orbicularis oris, works in the same way. Several other muscles in the face are not attached to bones. They pull on each other. This is how we make our huge range of facial expressions.

Most muscles are attached to bones. They rarely work alone. They pull in pairs or teams to make a bone move in a precise way. One bone may have 20 or 30 muscles attached to it, each in a different place and pulling in a different direction. This means different combinations of muscles can tilt and twist the bone in almost any direction, as when you turn your outstretched arm and hand from palm-up to palm-down.

The body has different types of muscle in the walls of its inner organs, such as the intestines and bladder, and in the heart.

When you hit a tennis ball, this involves more than one hundred muscles in your shoulder, arm, wrist, and hand. It also involves many other muscles all over the body. The other arm moves to keep you balanced. The middle of your body tilts forward to give the stroke extra power. The feet move up onto tiptoe and one leg steps forward as you complete the stroke. By the end, almost every muscle has been used.

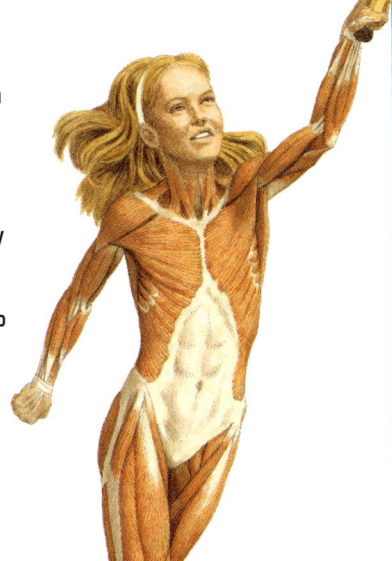

Skin

THE LARGEST part of the human body is its outer covering—the skin. This is like a flexible, all-over coat that protects the body from knocks and keeps out dirt and germs. It also keeps the delicate inner parts of the body moist and shields them from the harmful rays of the sun. Skin is at its thickest, two-tenths of an inch (5 mm) or more, on the soles of the feet. The thinnest skin, about two-hundredths of an inch (0.5 mm), is on the eyelids.

Skin gives the body its sense of touch. Millions of microscopic nerve endings just under the surface detect light touch, heavy pressure, heat, cold, and pain. The skin grows hairs from tiny pits called follicles. There are about 120,000 large hairs on the head, and four million tiny hairs over the rest of the body. Skin also sweats and increases the amount of blood flowing through it, to keep the body cool in hot conditions.

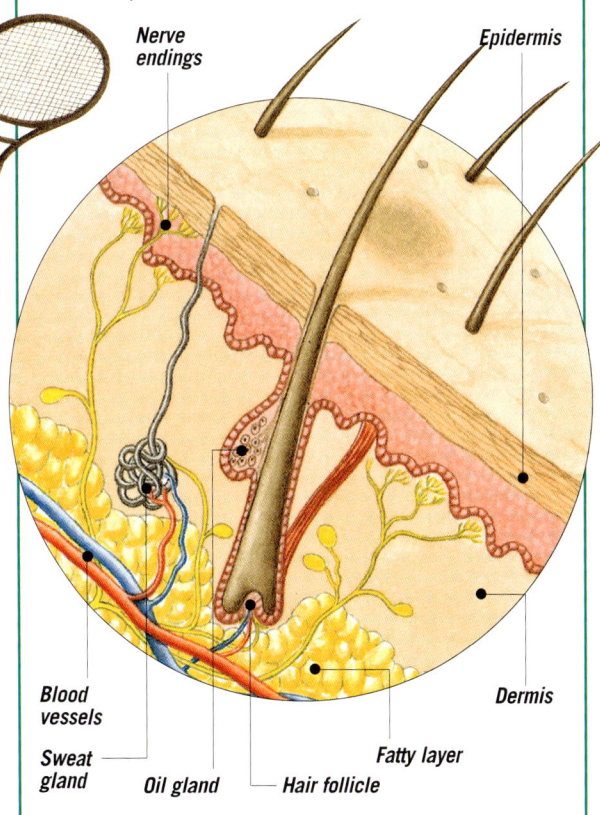

Nerve endings *Epidermis*
Blood vessels *Dermis*
Sweat gland *Oil gland* *Hair follicle* *Fatty layer*

This is a cross-section of skin, greatly enlarged. Skin has two layers. The upper epidermis continually renews itself as its hard, dead outer surface is worn away by daily activity. The much thicker lower layer, the dermis, contains nerves, blood vessels, sweat glands, and hair follicles.

45

HUMAN BODY

BONES AND JOINTS

THE 206 BONES of the body make up its skeleton *(see page 42)*. Each bone forms a hard, rigid inner support for its part of the body, and anchorage points for muscles to pull as the body moves. The old bones of a museum skeleton are dry, brittle, and crumbly. But inside the body, a bone is a very active, living part. It is not dry—it contains about one-fifth water. It is not brittle—it is slightly bendy because it contains fibers of a flexible substance, the body protein called collagen. Bone is also very tough because it contains hard crystals of minerals such as calcium phosphate. And like any other body part, a bone has a supply of blood vessels and nerves.

Most bones are not solid. They are hollow, with a cavity inside. This contains a soft, jellylike substance called bone marrow. The marrow makes new microscopic red and white cells for the blood at the rate of two million every second, to replace the old, dead blood cells.

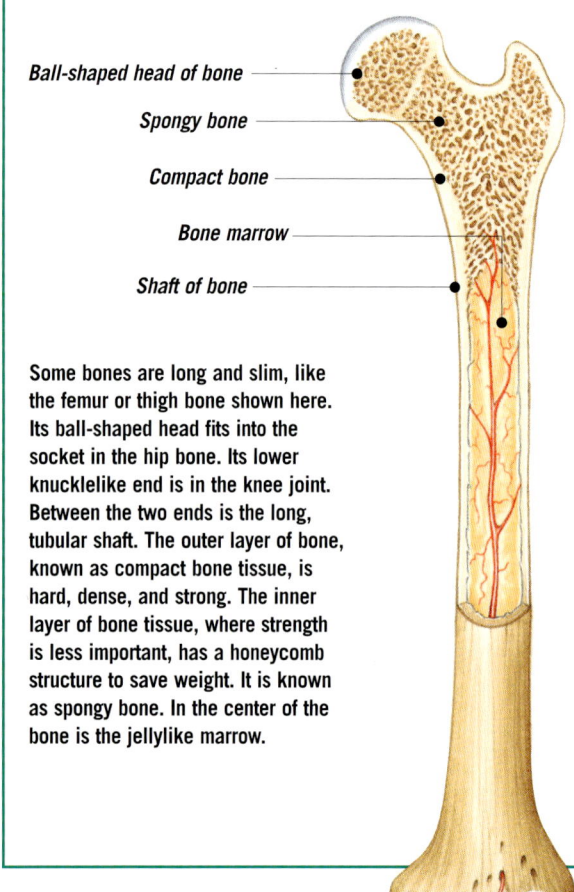

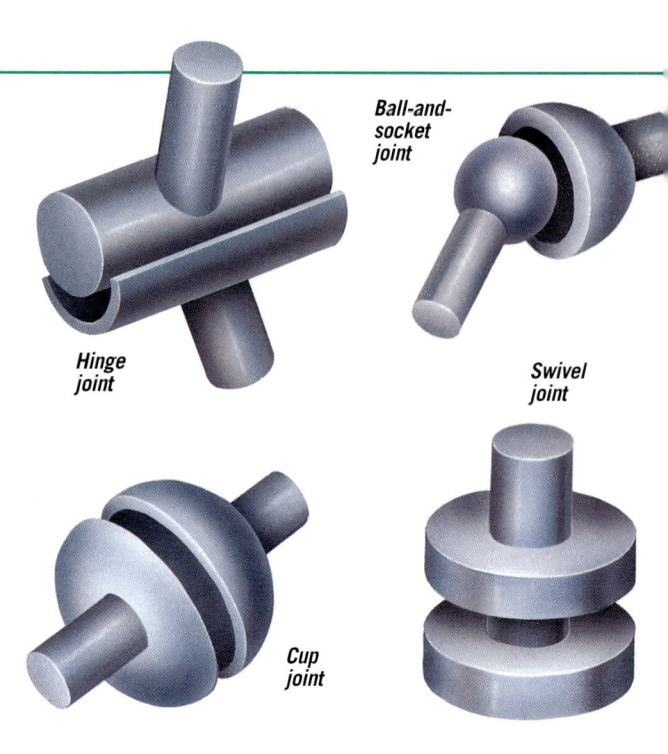

Hinge joint

Ball-and-socket joint

Swivel joint

Cup joint

TYPES OF JOINTS

Bones are linked together at joints. In some joints the bones are fixed or cemented firmly to each other and cannot move, as with the small bones of the face. These are known as suture joints. In other joints the bones can move in relation to each other. The body has many different kinds of moveable joints, depending on the shapes of the bone ends and how they fit together. They resemble the joints used in machines to give a certain kind of movement *(see above)*. For example, the knee is a hinge joint and moves only backward and forward. The hip is a ball-and-socket joint and can move in any direction.

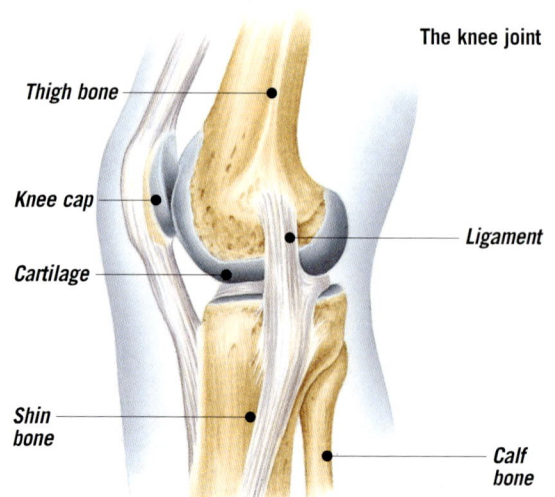

Ball-shaped head of bone
Spongy bone
Compact bone
Bone marrow
Shaft of bone

Some bones are long and slim, like the femur or thigh bone shown here. Its ball-shaped head fits into the socket in the hip bone. Its lower knucklelike end is in the knee joint. Between the two ends is the long, tubular shaft. The outer layer of bone, known as compact bone tissue, is hard, dense, and strong. The inner layer of bone tissue, where strength is less important, has a honeycomb structure to save weight. It is known as spongy bone. In the center of the bone is the jellylike marrow.

The knee joint
Thigh bone
Knee cap
Cartilage
Ligament
Shin bone
Calf bone

46

HUMAN BODY

Inside the knee joint

Synovial fluid

Cartilage within joint

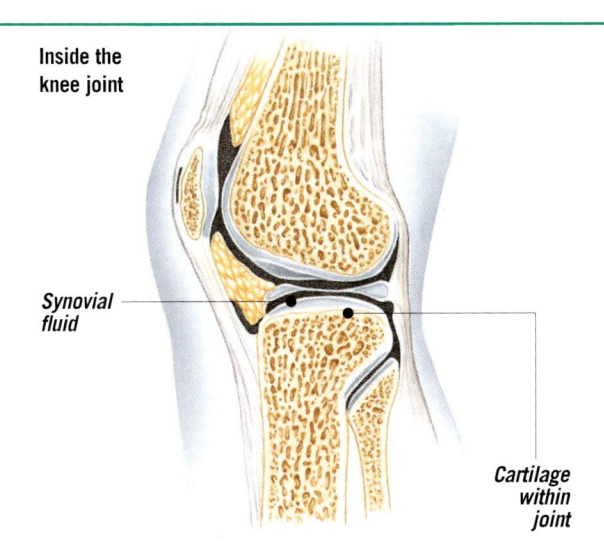

INSIDE A JOINT

In a moveable joint the ends of the bones are covered with a smooth, shiny, slippery, slightly soft substance called cartilage. This prevents the bone ends rubbing against each other and wearing away. The cartilage surfaces slip over each other with hardly any wear. A flexible bag, the synovial capsule, wraps around the bone ends. This makes an oily fluid which fills the bag and lubricates the joint, like the oil in a machine. The two bones are linked by flexible, straplike ligaments around the synovial capsule. These stop the bones coming apart and prevent the joint bending too much.

The hip region has both fixed and moveable joints. The hip bone is, in fact, six separate bones joined firmly together and to the sacrum at the base of the spine. The joint at the front, the pubic symphysis, has cartilage between the bones and can bend slightly. Ball-and-socket joints allow the legs a wide range of movement.

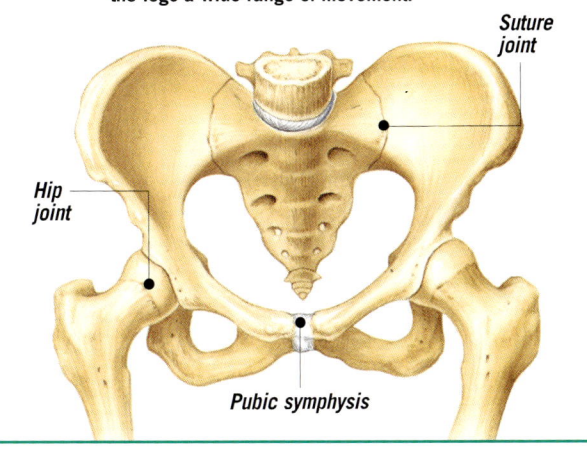

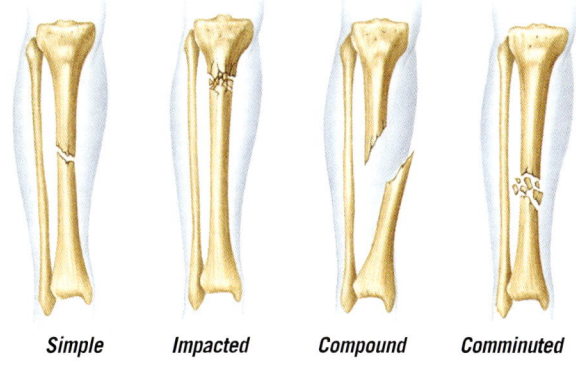

Suture joint

Hip joint

Pubic symphysis

Simple   **Impacted**   **Compound**   **Comminuted**

FRACTURES

Bones are strong but sometimes they cannot withstand the stress put on them, especially in an accident. A bone may crack or snap. This is known as a fracture. In a compound fracture, the broken ends protrude through the skin *(above)*. Part of the bone shatters into small parts in a comminuted fracture. The parts of the bone ram into each other in an impacted fracture.

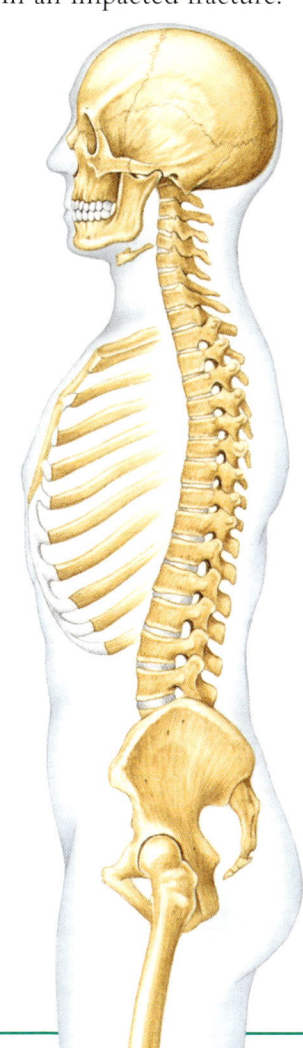

The backbone or spinal column (spine) is made of 26 separate bones called the vertebrae. Each is linked to bones above and below by a simple ringlike joint, except at the top where specialized joints with the skull allow the head to nod and twist. A pad of cartilage between each pair of vertebrae, known as the intervertebral disc, provides a flexible cushion so that the vertebrae can twist and tilt slightly against each other. Over the whole backbone, these limited movements add up so that the spine can bend into a U-shape.

HUMAN BODY

THE BRAIN

EVERY THOUGHT and idea, every wish and want, every emotion and feeling, happens inside the brain. The brain fills the top half of the head, well protected within the domed skull bone. It looks like a large, wrinkled lump of pink-gray jelly. It contains some 50 billion nerve cells, or neurons *(see opposite)*. Each nerve cell is linked to many thousands of others. Tiny electrical nerve signals pass through this vast network, representing your thoughts and memories. Nerve signals also come into the brain from nerves all over the body, and go out to the muscles.

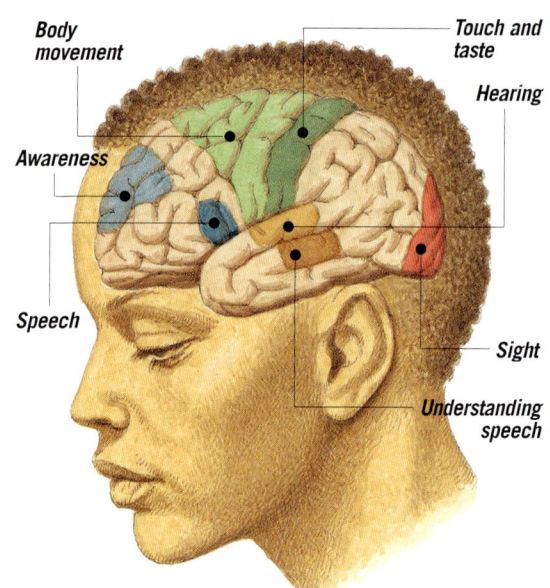

The large, wrinkled cerebrum makes up four-fifths of the brain's bulk. Its outer layer, about one- to two-tenths of an inch thick, is called the cerebral cortex. This is where most thoughts and ideas occur. The cortex has different areas called centers that deal with nerve signals coming from and going to different body parts *(above)*. For example, signals from the eyes are sorted and analyzed in the sight center at the lower rear of the brain. A slice through the brain shows its inner parts *(left)*. The hypothalamus monitors conditions within the body, such as the level of oxygen in the blood. It sends signals to the pituitary gland just below it, which controls the body's hormone system *(see page 51)*.

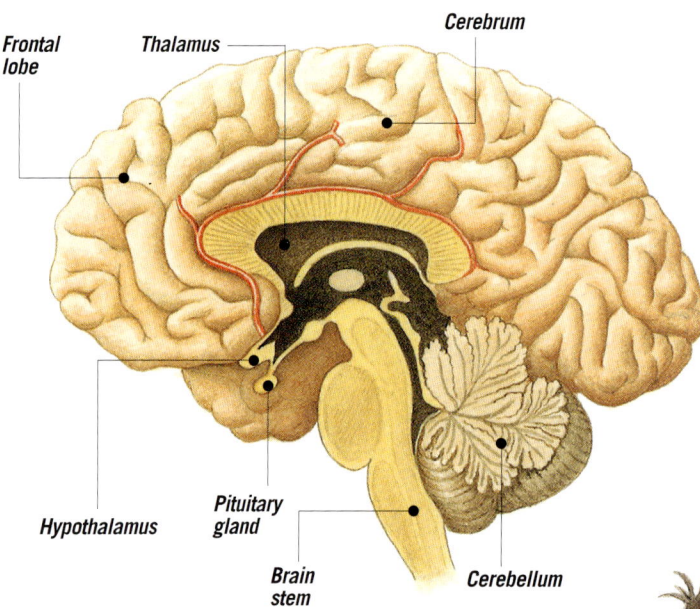

INSIDE THE BRAIN

The brain has four main parts. The brain stem at the base tapers into the spinal cord *(see opposite)*. It controls automatic bodily activities such as heartbeat, breathing, and digestion. The mid-brain just above has close links with the hormone system *(see page 51)*. One of its parts, the thalamus, controls the level of awareness, from wide awake and alert to drowsy or asleep. The third part is the cerebellum, a wrinkled lump at the rear. It deals with muscle control to make movements smooth and coordinated. The fourth part is the cerebrum, where thinking happens.

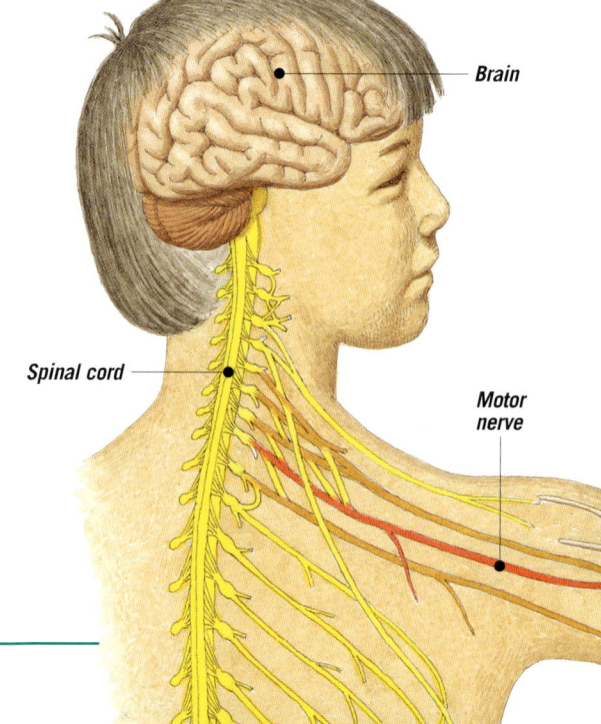

48

HUMAN BODY

NERVE CELLS AND SIGNALS

A nerve signal is a tiny pulse of electricity that travels very fast, almost 333 feet (100.6 m) per second, along a nerve cell. A nerve cell *(below)* has a normal-shaped cell body surrounded by thin, spidery parts called dendrites. It also has a very long, thin part like a wire, called the axon. Dendrites collect nerve signals from other nerve cells and pass them on, via the axon, to other nerve cells. Nerves contain bundles of hundreds or thousands of nerve cells.

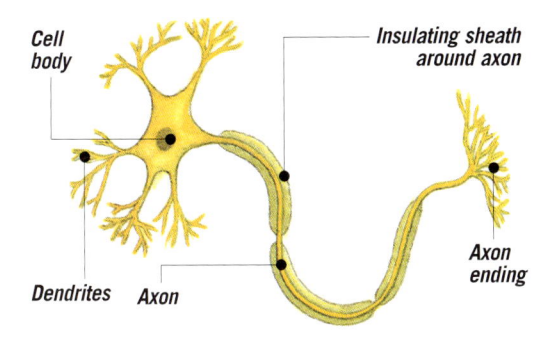

Cell body — **Insulating sheath around axon**
Dendrites **Axon** **Axon ending**

The brain's thoughts, ideas, and memories consist of nerve signals flashing to and fro around the unimaginably vast network of billions of nerve cells. New connections between nerve cells are constantly being made as old ones are lost. A new memory may form as a new pathway or route around certain cells. If you recall this memory often, you "refresh" the pathway and keep it active. If not, the memory fades.

A reflex is a fast, automatic movement that your body makes by itself, without your brain having to think about it. If you touch something sharp, pain sensors in the skin send nerve signals along sensory nerves in the arm to the spinal cord in the back. Signals go straight out again along motor nerves to the arm muscles, to make your arm pull away. A split second later signals go up to the brain, so that you become aware of what has happened.

Sensory nerve

THE NERVOUS SYSTEM

The base of the brain merges into the spinal cord. The cord has nerve branches that reach out to every body part, down to the fingertips and toes. The spinal cord carries nerve signals between the brain and all of these body parts. In addition, there are nerves that branch directly from the brain, into the head, face, neck, and chest. These are cranial nerves.

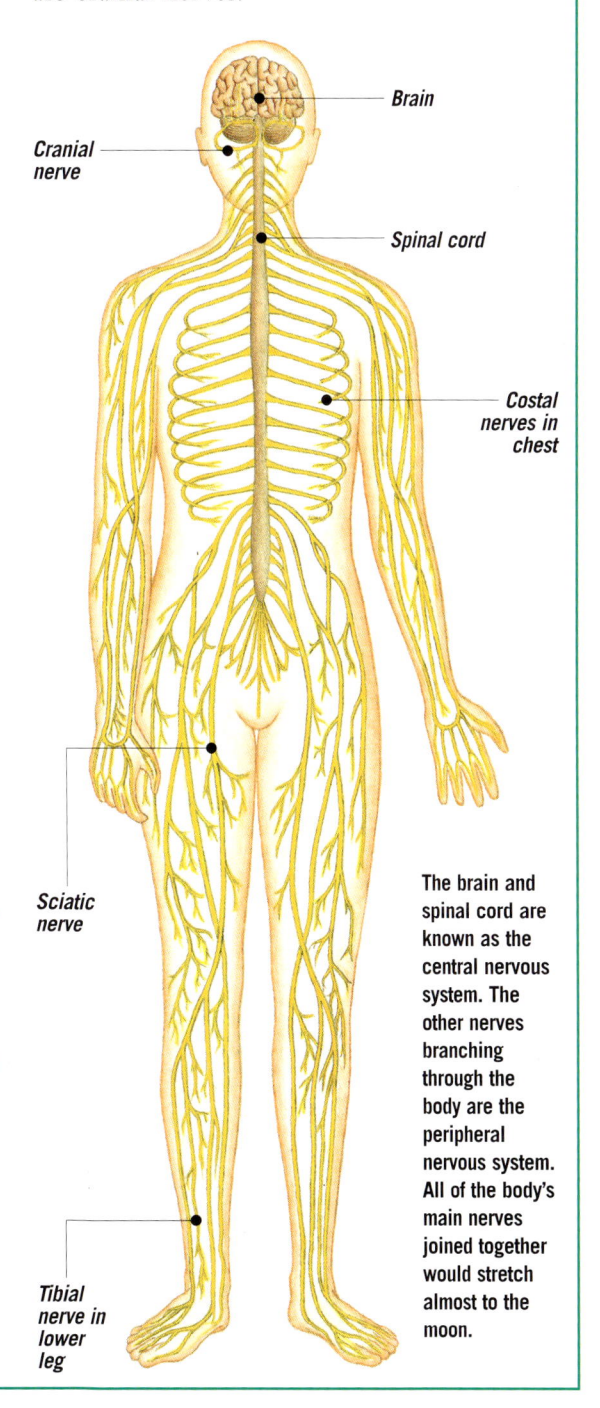

Brain
Cranial nerve
Spinal cord
Costal nerves in chest
Sciatic nerve
Tibial nerve in lower leg

The brain and spinal cord are known as the central nervous system. The other nerves branching through the body are the peripheral nervous system. All of the body's main nerves joined together would stretch almost to the moon.

49

HUMAN BODY

THE SENSES

THE BODY has five main senses that detect what is happening in the outside world. Four are shown here. The fifth is touch, sensed by the skin *(see page 45)*.

SIGHT

Each eyeball is about one inch (25 mm) across and well protected in a socket, called the orbit, inside the skull bone. Light rays enter the eye through its transparent domed front, the cornea. They pass into the eye through the pupil, a hole in a ring of muscle known as the iris. The iris makes the pupil smaller in bright conditions, to prevent too much light damaging the eye's delicate interior. The rays are bent or focused by the lens, and shine a clear image onto the retina, which lines the rear of the eyeball. When light hits the retina, its 130 million microscopic cells make nerve signals, which pass along the optic nerve to the brain.

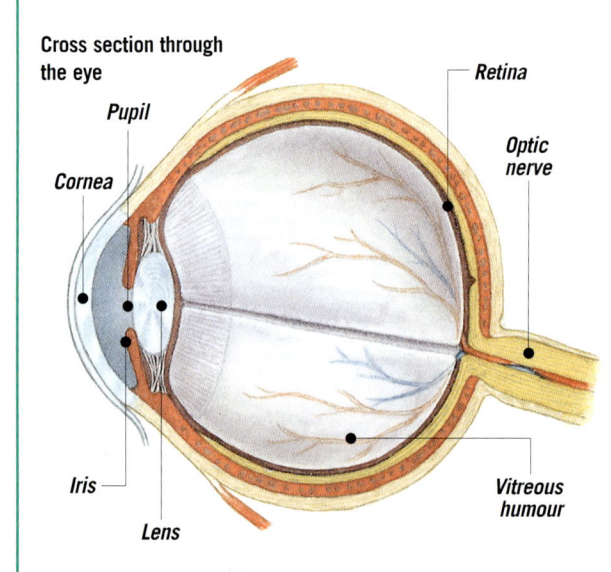

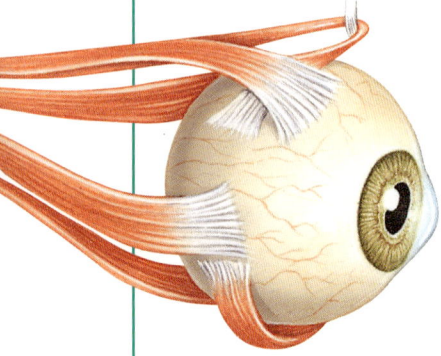

Cross section through the eye
- Pupil
- Cornea
- Iris
- Lens
- Retina
- Optic nerve
- Vitreous humour

Most of the eye's interior is filled with a see-through jelly called the vitreous humor *(above)*. Light shines through this onto the retina. Six small strap-shaped muscles attach the eyeball to the rear of the eye socket *(left)*. They work together to make the eye look up, down, and sideways.

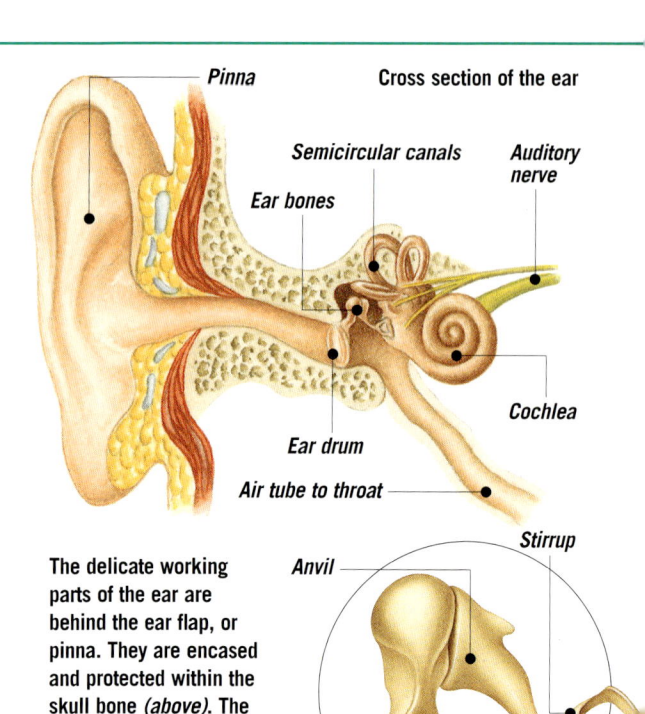

Cross section of the ear
- Pinna
- Semicircular canals
- Ear bones
- Auditory nerve
- Cochlea
- Ear drum
- Air tube to throat
- Stirrup
- Anvil
- Hammer

The delicate working parts of the ear are behind the ear flap, or pinna. They are encased and protected within the skull bone *(above)*. The three tiny ear bones, or auditory ossicles, are the smallest bones in the body *(right)*.

HEARING

The curly flap of skin and gristle on the side of the head, which we call the ear, is simply a funnel shape for collecting sound waves from the air around. The waves travel along a slightly curved tube, the ear canal, and strike the ear drum, a small, thin piece of skin, which vibrates. The vibrations pass along a row of three tiny bones, the hammer, anvil, and stirrup. The stirrup sends the vibrations into a snail-shaped part filled with fluid, known as the cochlea. The vibrations ripple through the fluid and shake microscopic hairs sticking out of nerve cells. When the hairs shake, the cells produce nerve signals, which travel along the auditory nerve to the brain.

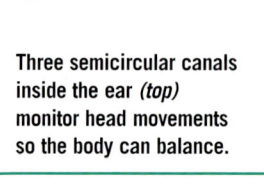

Three semicircular canals inside the ear *(top)* monitor head movements so the body can balance.

HUMAN BODY

TASTE

The tongue's upper surface is covered with many pimplelike lumps, known as papillae. These grip food to move it around while chewing. Scattered between the papillae are about 8,000 taste buds. Each one has some 30 microscopic taste cells and looks like a tiny onion set into the tongue's surface. When substances of a certain flavor in foods touch micro-hairs sticking up from the taste cells, the cells generate nerve signals which pass to the brain. Different tongue areas respond to different flavors.

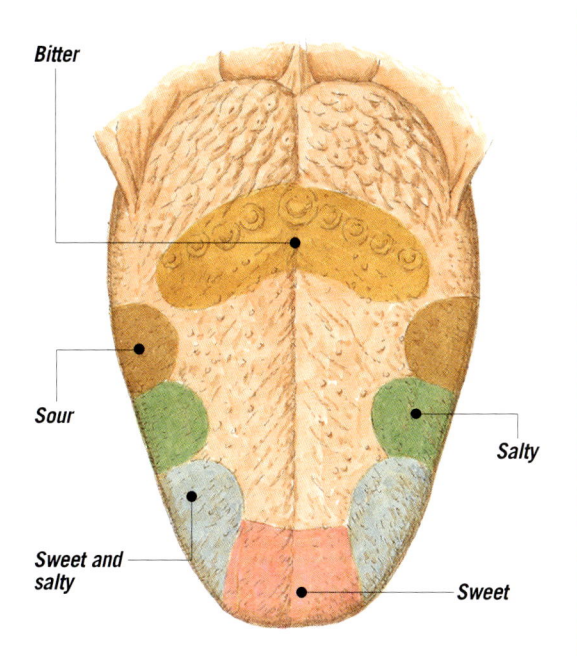

Bitter

Sour

Salty

Sweet and salty

Sweet

SMELL

In each side of the nose is an air chamber about as large as a thumb. Lining the roof of the chamber is a patch of 25 million smell cells. Each has more than 20 tiny hairs sticking from it. When certain odor substances touch the hairs, their cells send nerve signals to the brain. The nose can detect 10,000 different scents and smells.

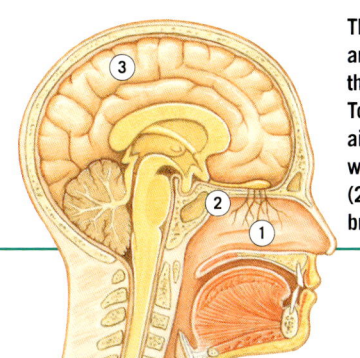

The olfactory (smell) area lies at the top of the nasal cavity (1). To smell, we sniff the air into this area, where olfactory nerves (2) send signals to the brain (3).

HORMONES

TWO SYSTEMS help the body's parts and organs work together. One is the nervous system *(see page 49)*. The other is the hormonal or endocrine system, based on body chemicals called hormones. There are more than 50 different hormones. Each is made in a gland. Hormones flow around the bloodstream and affect certain cells, tissues and organs. They may cause them to work faster or slower, or release their products. For example, adrenaline from the adrenal gland makes the heart beat faster and more blood flow to the muscles, so the body is ready for action. The pituitary gland near the brain makes hormones that control other hormonal glands *(see also page 54)*.

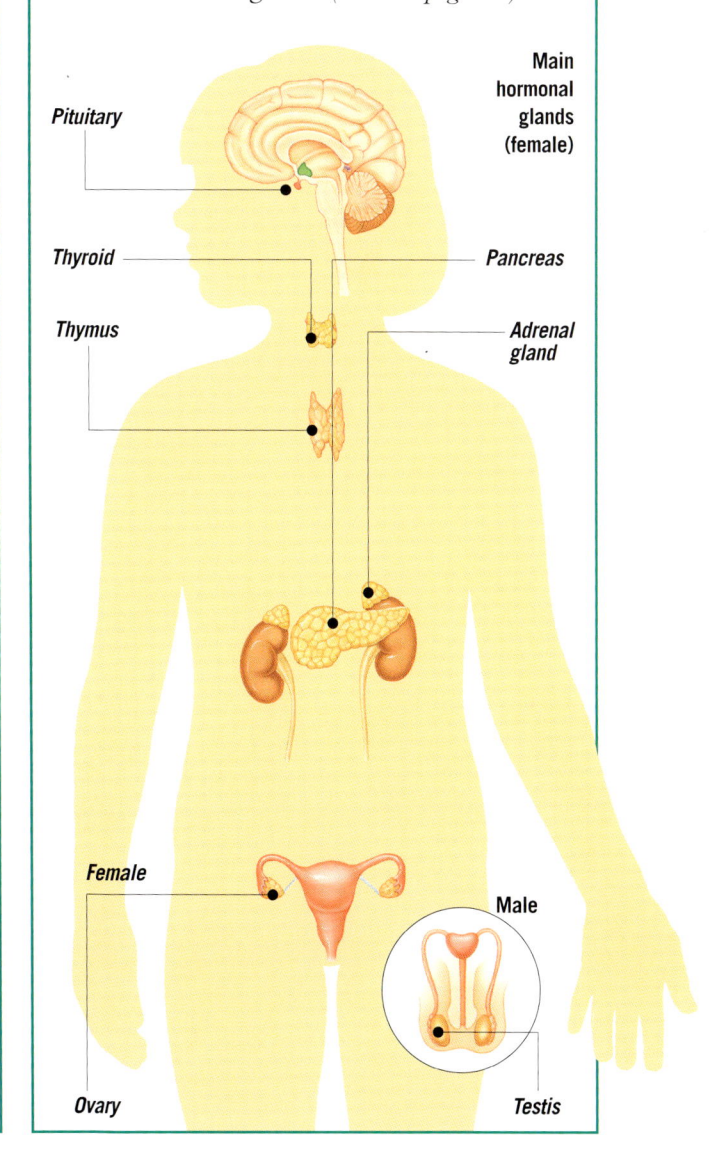

Main hormonal glands (female)

Pituitary

Thyroid

Thymus

Pancreas

Adrenal gland

Female

Male

Ovary

Testis

HUMAN BODY

CELLS AND GENES

THE BASIC "building blocks" of the body are cells. There are over 200 different types, such as blood cells, nerve cells, and muscle fiber cells. They vary greatly in size and shape, although most cells are far too small to see except through a powerful microscope. About 30 typical cells placed in a row would stretch only four-hundredths of an inch (1mm). The whole body contains more than 50 million million cells. Most are in the blood and the brain.

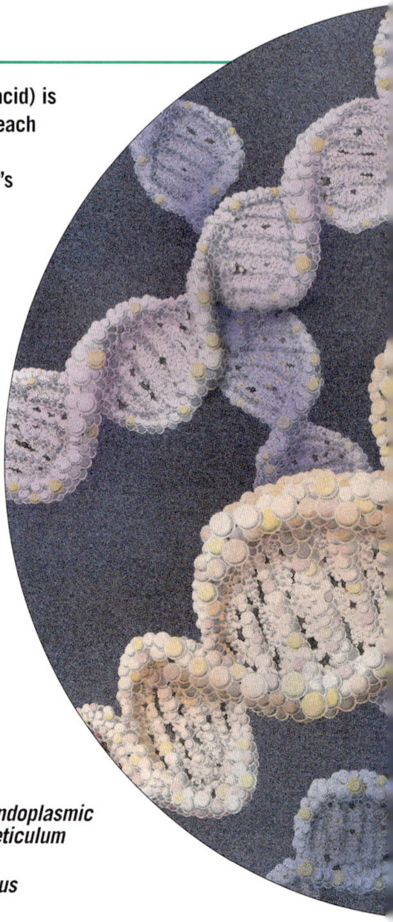

DNA (deoxyribonucleic acid) is found in the nucleus of each cell. It is the chemical which contains the body's genes. A piece or molecule of DNA is enormously long and thin, like a rope ladder twisted into a corkscrew shape. All the DNA in one cell nucleus joined together would stretch nearly 6.5 feet (2 m).

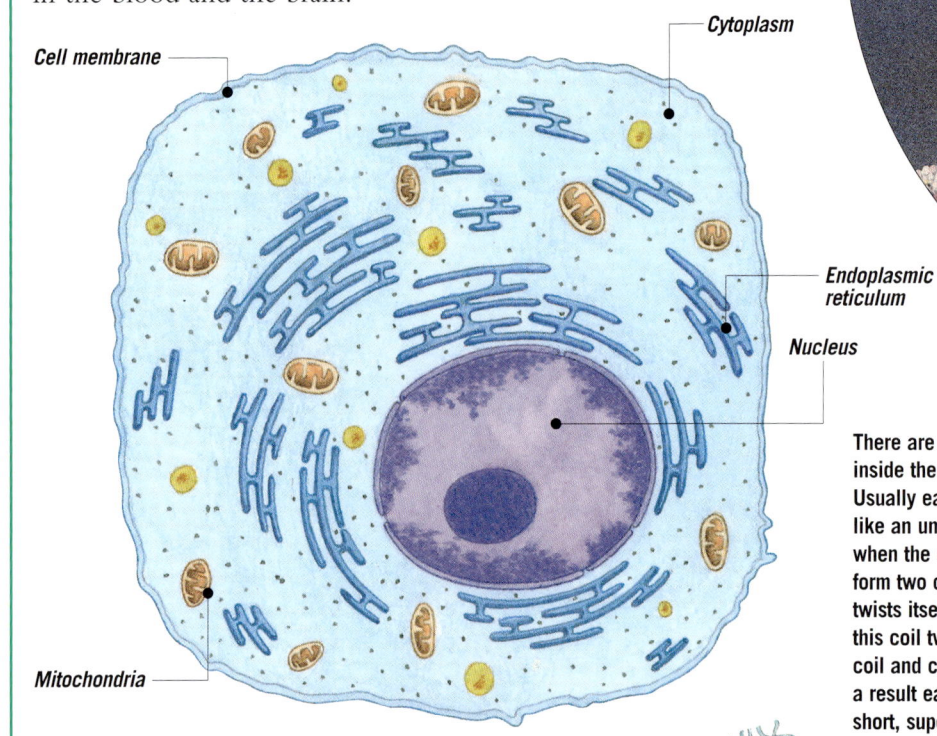

Cell membrane
Cytoplasm
Endoplasmic reticulum
Nucleus
Mitochondria

There are 46 main pieces of DNA inside the nucleus of one cell. Usually each piece is spread out like an unwound length of rope. But when the cell is about to divide and form two cells, each length of DNA twists itself into a tight coil. In turn, this coil twists itself into a super-coil and combines with protein. As a result each length of DNA forms a short, super-coiled bundle called a chromosome *(see page 55)*.

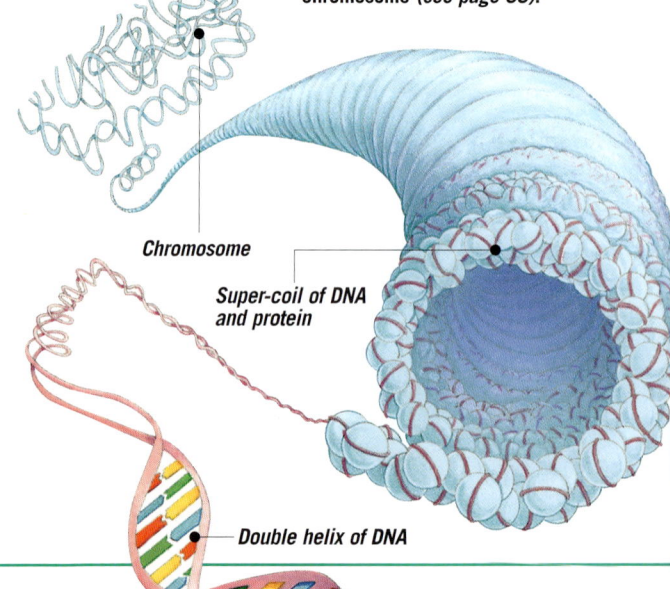

INSIDE A CELL

A typical cell is a bag of jelly, or cytoplasm, containing even smaller parts called organelles *(above)*. Mitochondria are small and sausage-shaped. They break up substances such as sugar (glucose) to release energy for use in the cell. The cell's skinlike covering, the cell membrane, allows only certain substances to pass in and out. The cell's factory for making various substances and products is called the endoplasmic reticulum. The biggest organelle is usually the nucleus, a dark lump near the cell's center. It contains genes in the form of DNA.

Chromosome
Super-coil of DNA and protein
Double helix of DNA

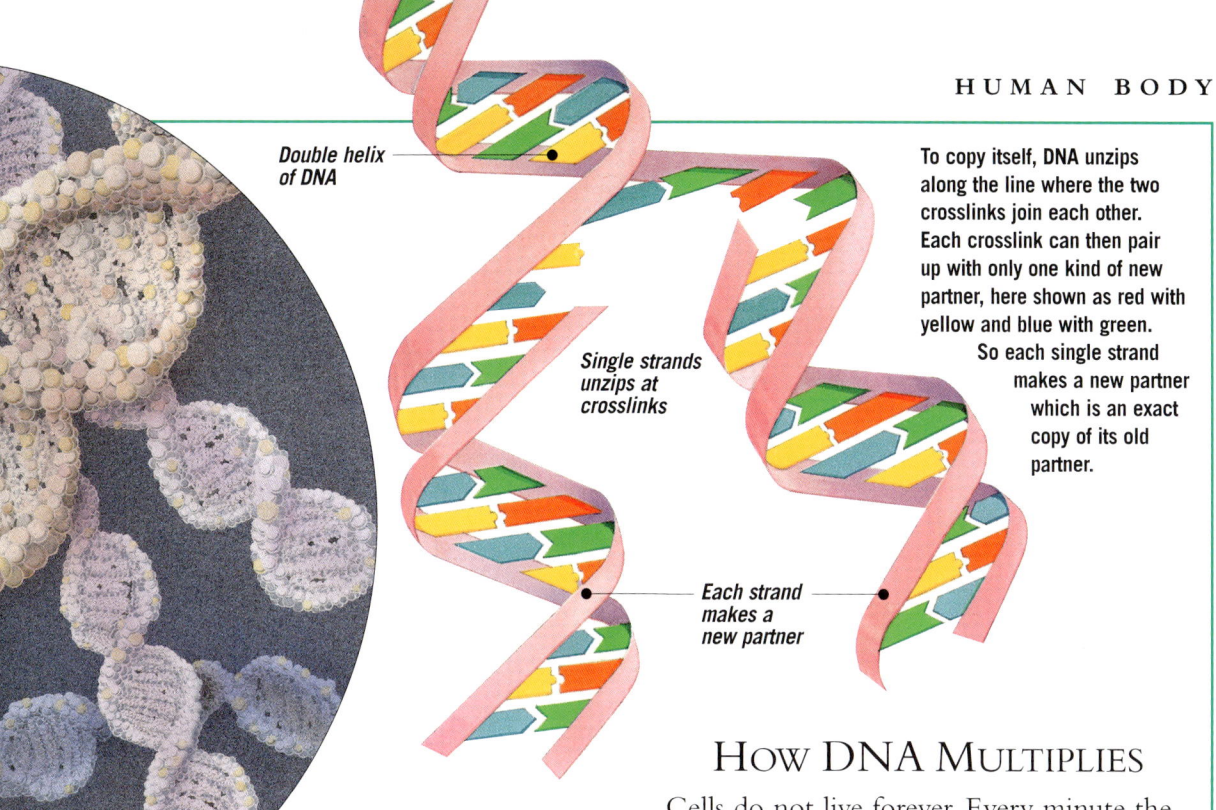

HUMAN BODY

Double helix of DNA

Single strands unzips at crosslinks

To copy itself, DNA unzips along the line where the two crosslinks join each other. Each crosslink can then pair up with only one kind of new partner, here shown as red with yellow and blue with green. So each single strand makes a new partner which is an exact copy of its old partner.

Each strand makes a new partner

How DNA Multiplies

Cells do not live forever. Every minute the body makes about 3,000 million new cells to replace those which naturally wear out and die. Also, reproduction involves making new cells *(see page 54)*. When a cell divides to make two new cells, its set of DNA is copied to make a duplicate set. Then each of the two new cells has a full DNA set with all the genes. DNA duplicates (copies) itself by breaking the crosslinks that hold together its two strands. Each nucleotide subunit then joins to a new partner of its usual kind—A with T, and G with C. The row of new subunits forms its own new strand. The result is two lengths of DNA, each identical to the other.

Genes contain all the information a living thing needs to develop, grow, and maintain itself through life. A tiny worm has a few hundred genes. The human body has more than 100,000 genes. They determine whether you have dark hair, long legs, a tendency to develop certain diseases, and so on.

Genes are encoded like an "instruction manual" in DNA. The twisted-ladder shape of DNA is called a double helix. The rungs or crosslinks are made of chemical subunits, known as nucleotides. There are four: A, T, G, and C (adenine, thymine, guanine, and cytosine). A always forms a crosslink with T, and G with C. The order of subunits A, T, G, and C along the DNA is the genetic code, containing information for the genes in chemical form. Every body cell has a full set of DNA including all genes. But each cell uses only a tiny part of the DNA for its own life processes.

If two bodies have the same genes, they look the same. This happens with identical twins *(right)*. They both develop from the same fertilized egg cell which splits in two *(see next page)*. Nonidentical twins are produced when two eggs are both fertilized. Identical twins will always be of the same sex and have the same eye color.

53

HUMAN BODY

REPRODUCTION

THE KEY FEATURE of all living things is that they can make more of their kind. This is called reproduction. The human body reproduces in much the same way as animals such as cats, dogs, horses, and tigers. A female and male come together and have sexual intercourse. A microscopic tadpole-shaped cell from the male joins with, or fertilizes, an egg cell from the female. This fertilized egg grows and develops in the womb of the female, into a baby ready to be born.

The main parts of the female reproductive system are the two ovaries and the womb. They are in the lower body; the pear-shaped womb positioned just behind the bladder. Once each month during the menstrual cycle (the female reproductive cycle), one ovary releases a pinhead-sized egg cell. This passes into the egg duct, where it may join with a sperm. The menstrual cycle is controlled by hormones.

The main parts of the male reproductive system are the two testes. They make millions of tiny sperm cells each day. The sperm are stored in a long coiled tube, the epididymis. During sex they pass along the sperm duct, mix with fluid from the seminal vesicle and prostate gland, and travel along the urethra. They pass out of the end of the penis, into the woman's body.

SEX ORGANS

The parts of the body involved in reproduction are called the sex organs *(above and above left)*. They are present at birth, but they develop rapidly and start to work from the ages of about 11 to 14 years in girls and 13 to 16 years in boys. This time of rapid growth and changes in bodily features is known as puberty. A girl develops a more rounded body outline and her breasts enlarge. A boy grows facial hair and his voice breaks. These changes are controlled by hormones *(see page 51)*.

HUMAN BODY

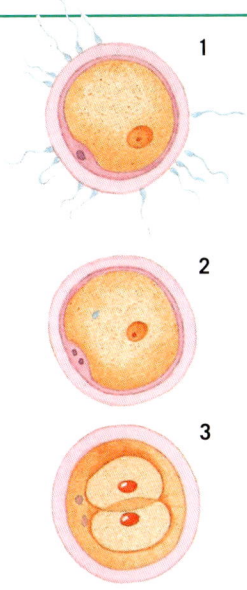

1 During sexual intercourse, a man releases many millions of sperm cells, which are much smaller than the egg cell. Each sperm has a round head and swims by lashing its long tail. The sperm move along the egg tube toward the egg. Several manage to reach it (1), but only one sperm cell joins, or fertilizes, the egg. The others are kept out as a thick barrier develops around the egg (2). The genes in the sperm and egg combine to form a single cell, the fertilized egg. Almost at once this divides by the process of cell division to form two cells (3).

A few hours after the fertilized egg divides into two cells, each of these cells also divides to make four cells (4). A few hours later the same happens to give eight cells, and so on. The result is a ball-shaped clump called a morula (5). About five days after fertilization, the morula has become a hollow ball known as a blastocyst with hundreds of cells (6). By this time it has passed along the egg tube into the womb. It has been living on nutrients stored in the original huge egg cell. Now it absorbs nutrients from the womb lining, so it can begin to grow.

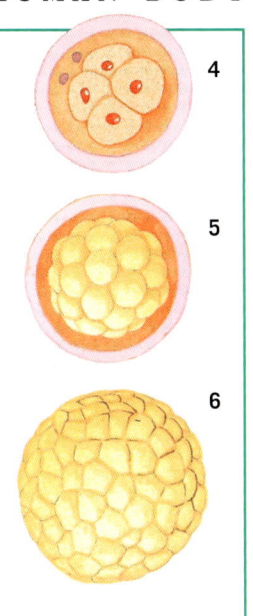

THE FIRST WEEK OF LIFE

The egg cell (ovum) contains a set of genetic material from the mother. The sperm cell (spermatozoon) has a set from the father. When sperm and egg join, the fertilized egg contains the normal double set of genetic material found in all body cells. The fertilized egg is larger than most cells, almost one-tenth of one millimeter across. But it divides many times *(above)* by the process of cell division *(below)*, so the cells reduce back to normal size. During this time the ball of cells passes along the egg duct to the womb.

The womb lining has become thickened and rich with blood and nutrients, as part of the menstrual cycle. When the ball of cells reaches the inside of the womb, it burrows into the lining. The cells in the ball continue to multiply and the ball becomes hollow. A flatter, disc-shaped part appears in the middle of the hollow ball. As the cells multiply into many thousands and begin to move about, the disc changes shape into a tiny, tadpolelike object. This is a very young baby, called an embryo. It is hardly larger than a grain of rice, but its heart is already beating. *(Continued on next page.)*

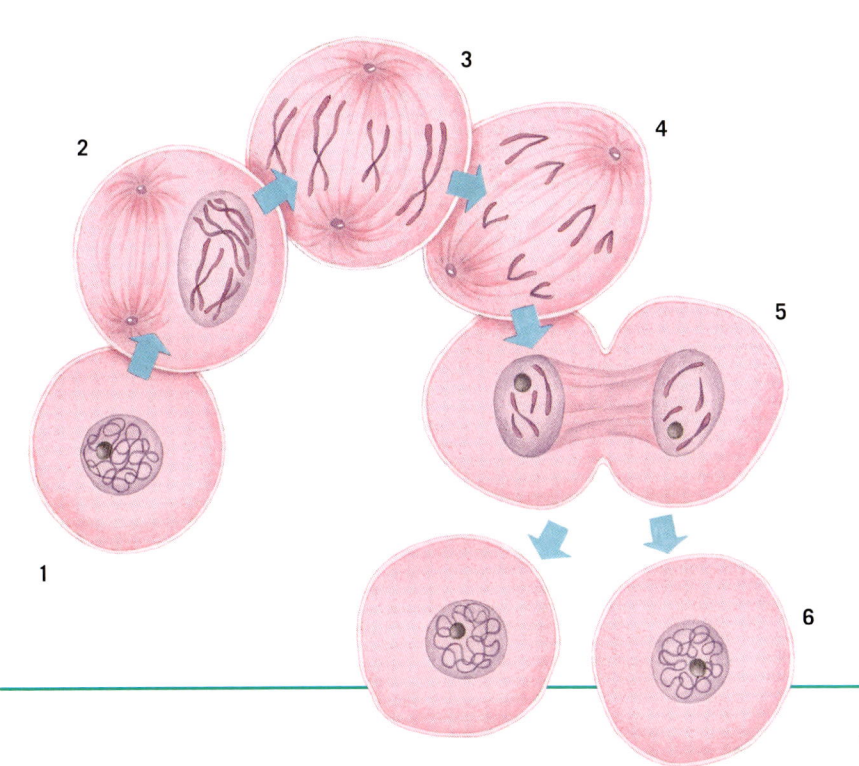

Cell division happens all over the body as cells wear away or die and need replacing. The genetic material, DNA, usually lies in long lengths inside the cell's nucleus (1). As division starts, the DNA coils into thicker, shorter objects called chromosomes (2). There are two of each chromosome. They line up across the middle of the cell (3) and are pulled by microthreads to opposite ends (4). A new nucleus forms around each set of chromosomes (5). Finally the original cell pinches into two new cells (6). The DNA in the chromosomes is copied and the cells grow larger before the next cell division *(see page 53)*.

A BABY GROWS

IT TAKES nine months for the fertilized egg to grow and develop in the mother's womb, then become a baby ready to be born. This time is known as pregnancy. For the first eight weeks the developing baby is called an embryo. During this period, all of the main body parts and organs, such as the brain, heart, eyes, ears, and even the fingers and toes, form. At the end of eight weeks, the embryo is only about the size of a thumb tip. But the main phase of development is complete and the baby looks like a miniature human being.

For the next seven months the main change is in size. The baby grows at a faster rate than it will ever grow in the rest of its life. Finishing touches are added to the body, such as fingernails, toenails, and eyelashes. During this growth phase the baby is known as a fetus.

EARLY DEVELOPMENT

The part of the baby that develops fastest is the head, followed by the main body and then the limbs. In the early stages, the brain and spinal cord are by far the largest part of the body *(see below)*. During the fourth week, the main body begins to develop. The heart pumps blood through a simple system of tubes and the lungs begin to grow.

Toward the end of the fourth week, the lower body organs, such as the intestine, liver, and pancreas, form. The arms and then the legs also start to develop. At first they are tiny bumps on the body called limb buds, but they soon lengthen and the fingers and toes take shape *(right)*.

During the fifth week, the ears, eyes, and nose take on more recognizable shapes. Main nerves begin to grow out from the brain and spinal cord. The kidneys and stomach also develop.

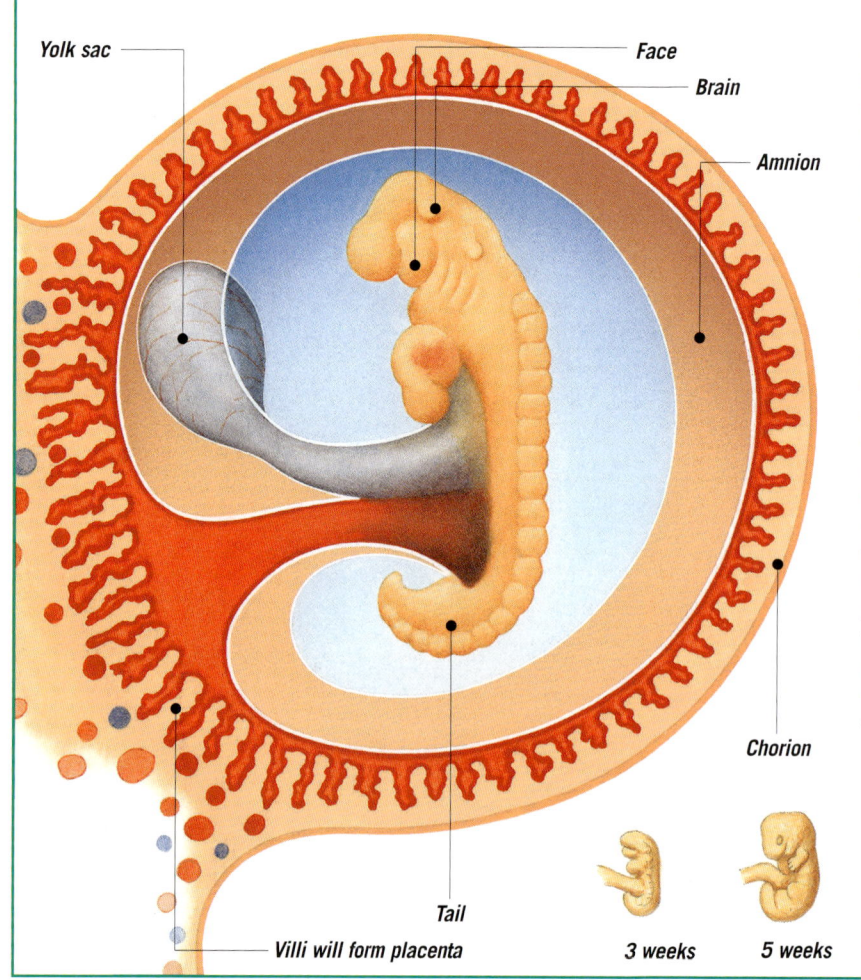

About three weeks after fertilization, the growing human embryo *(left)* looks much like the embryo of a dog, cat, or chicken at a similar stage *(see page 7)*. It even has a "tail," but this gradually shrinks away as growth continues. The largest part of the body is the brain and other developing areas of the head. The ridges along the back will eventually form the backbones (vertebrae), but proper bones do not start to develop until the third month. The embryo floats in fluid within skinlike outer membranes, the chorion and amnion. At this early stage it receives nutrients from the yolk sac. But parts of the outer membranes, called villi, are growing into the womb lining. They will form the placenta which provides nourishment *(above right)*. The stages of growth are shown life-sized *(below)*.

3 weeks   5 weeks   6 weeks   7 weeks

HUMAN BODY

Three months after fertilization, the baby is 2.5 inches (65 mm) long. Its ears are formed and can hear. The eyes are also formed, but the eyelids stay shut until nearer birth. The muscles are now starting to develop and the baby can twist and turn. The umbilical cord carries the baby's blood to the placenta where it flows very close to the mother's blood. In this way, the baby's blood collects nourishment and oxygen from the mother, while getting rid of its wastes to her blood.

Umbilical cord

Amniotic fluid

Placenta

Muscles of womb wall

5 weeks

7 weeks

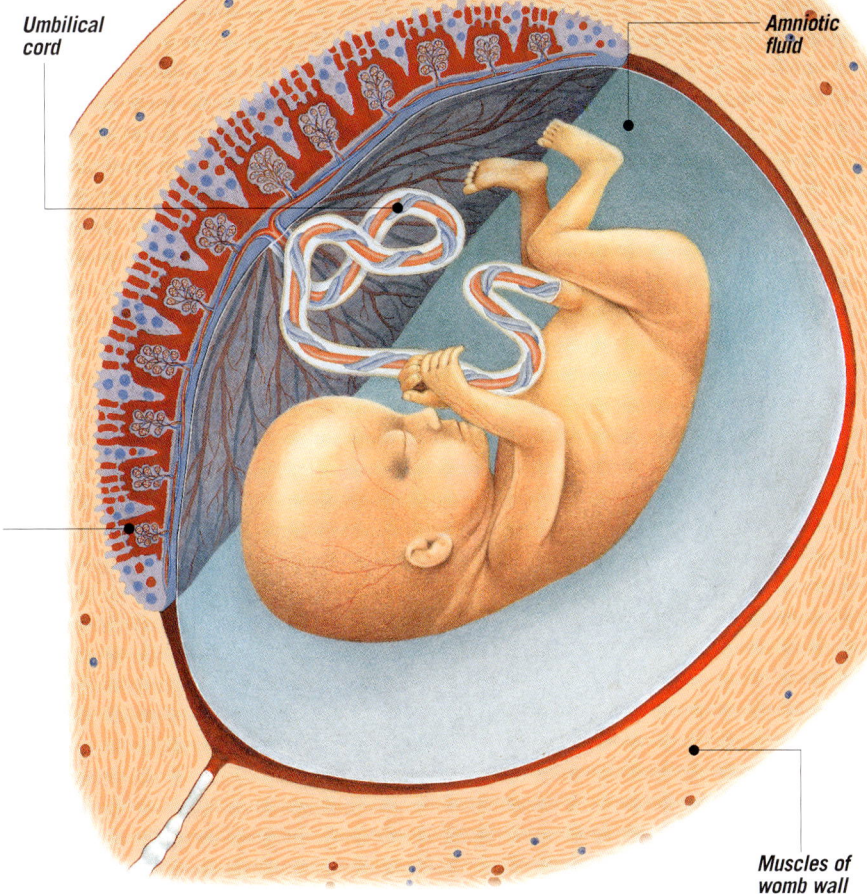

8 weeks

12 weeks

The fingers start to appear in the seventh week after fertilization. By the twelfth week they are fully formed and developing their fingernails. The toes grow in a similar way but lag a few days behind the fingers.

As the baby grows and the womb stretches to hold it, a "bump" appears on the mother's lower body. This usually becomes noticeable from about the fourth month of pregnancy. As the time for birth comes near, in the eighth month, the baby rests in a head-down position. When birth starts, the strong muscles in the womb wall push hard and squeeze the baby through the neck of the womb and along the birth canal. The baby emerges head-first. It is still attached by its umbilical cord to the placenta, and this emerges a short time later.

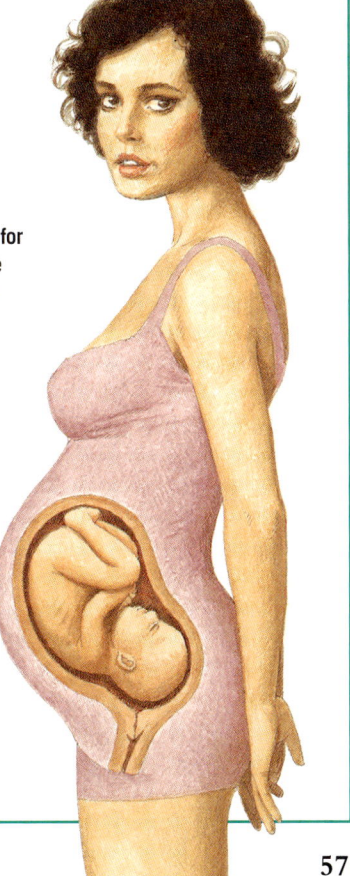

LIFE IN THE WOMB

Inside the womb, the baby floats in a pool of amniotic fluid. The fluid cushions and protects it from bumps and jolts. The baby cannot breathe or eat in its watery surroundings. So it receives oxygen and nutrients from the mother through the placenta (also called the afterbirth). The baby can hear sounds such as its mother's heartbeat. Loud noises from outside also pass into the womb and may startle the baby and make it jump. At first the baby has room to move and even turn somersaults. But as it grows larger it becomes more cramped, even though the womb stretches.

57

HUMAN BODY

MEDICINE

OCCASIONALLY the body is ill or suffers injury. From ancient times people have used many different methods—not always successfully—to help the sick and injured. Modern medicine is based on scientific tests and treatments rather than superstition or magic.

The common cold is a disease caused by a variety of viruses. Symptoms include a runny nose, sore throat, headache, sneezing, and coughing. Healthy people can carry cold-producing viruses for long periods.

Some diseases are carried in genes *(see page 53)* and inherited by later generations. Queen Victoria *(inset, top left)* passed on to several of her grandchildren, including the son of Nicholas II, tsar of Russia *(above)*, a disease called hemophilia, a condition where blood will not clot after injury.

Two main types of treatment are medical and surgical. Medical help involves chemicals or drugs. These may be obtained from natural substances such as plants, animals, or microbes, or made in the laboratory (for example, chemotherapy, used to fight cancer). Surgery involves physical treatment, for example, cutting open the body during an operation to remove a diseased part or mend a broken bone.

CLEAN CONDITIONS

Before the invention of the microscope, no one could see germs. These are microscopic life-forms such as bacteria and viruses that invade the body and cause the illnesses known as infections. Since people did not know about germs, they did not understand the importance of keeping wounds clean. Surgeons never bothered to wash their hands or their instruments. Many more people died after operations than got better.

In vaccinations, dead or disabled versions of germs are injected into the body. The germs cannot cause harm, but the body's defense system fights and kills them. It will then recognize the germs again quickly in the future. If real germs were to try to enter the body, they would be killed before they could cause illness. Protecting the body in this way is called immunization. It was first tried in a scientific form in 1796 by English doctor Edward Jenner (1749–1823) and soon became widespread. By 1980 the disease smallpox had been wiped out due to a worldwide campaign of vaccination.

HUMAN BODY

DOCTORS AND HOSPITALS

A doctor is qualified to examine and treat people using drugs and surgery. A person who is ill usually goes to the family doctor or general practitioner (GP). The GP has a wide knowledge of medicine and can diagnose (identify) and treat most illnesses.

If the cause of the problem is not clear, the person may be sent, or referred, to a hospital doctor or consultant. The consultant is an expert in a certain type of medicine. For example, a neurologist deals with problems of the brain and nerves and a cardiologist with diseases of the heart.

Emergency case

Operating theater

EMERGENCY MEDICINE

Some of the greatest advances in recent years have been in emergency medicine. When a person is badly injured in a road accident or suffers a heart attack, every second may count. The ambulance crew are specially trained and equipped to give life-saving first aid and to care for the victim or patient on the way to hospital.

At the hospital the patient is taken to ER (the emergency room) where specialist doctors quickly decide on treatment. If an emergency operation is needed, the surgeon and team go to the operating room or theater and begin right away. After surgery, the patient is looked after in ICU (the intensive care unit). Machines and monitors check the patient's heartbeat, breathing, blood pressure, and other body processes. If all goes well, the patient begins to recover and can leave ICU for the general ward. Nurses carry out daily care and check on progress until the patient is well enough to go home.

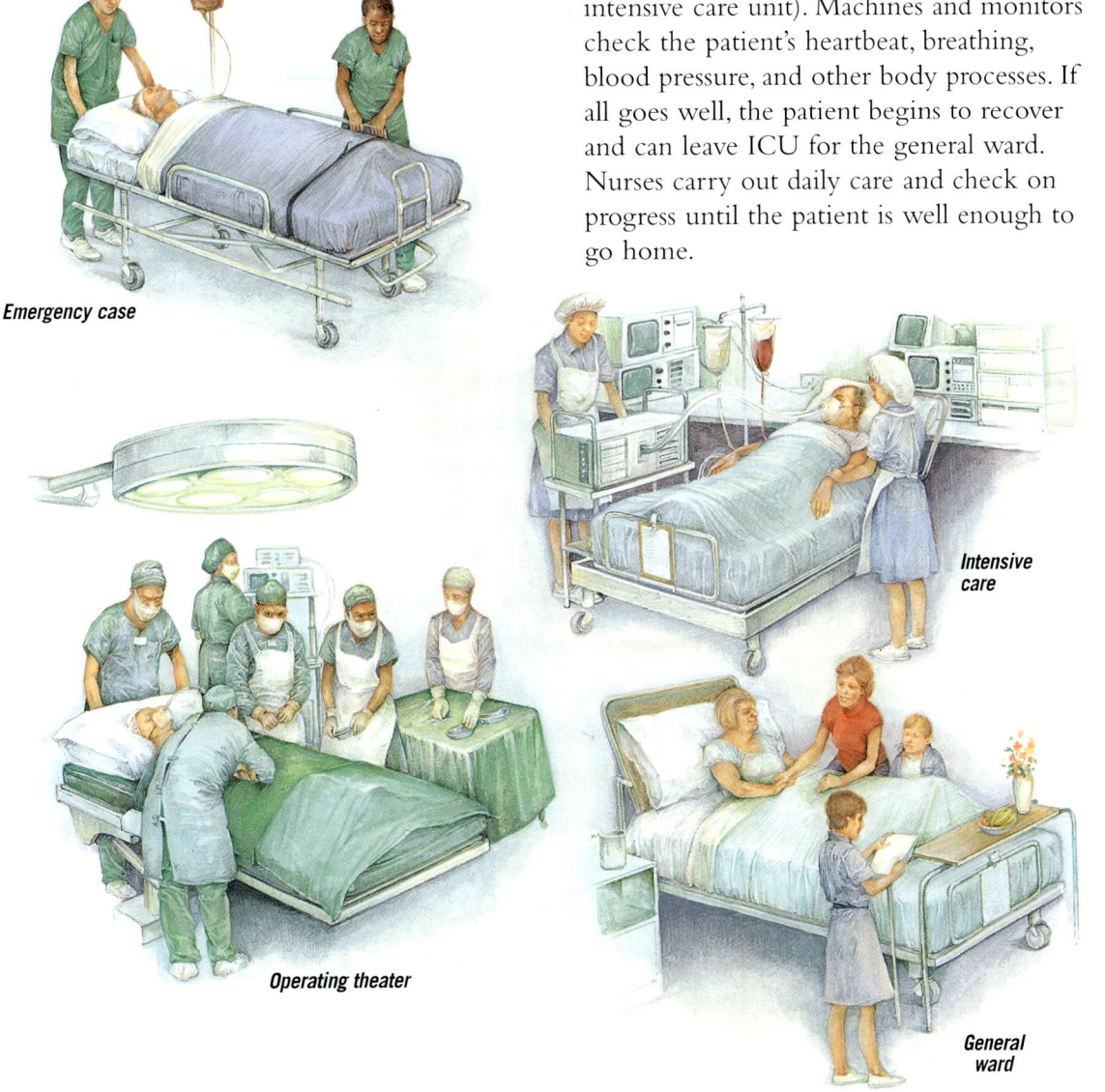

Intensive care

General ward

Glossary

Alveoli Tiny air sacs in the lungs where oxygen is taken up by the blood and carbon dioxide is released into the lungs and breathed out.

Antibody A substance carried in the blood that helps destroy bacteria and viruses.

Artery A tube that carries blood away from the heart. Most carry oxygen-rich blood to the body's organs and tissues but the pulmonary arteries, which run from the heart to the lungs, carry blood with very little oxygen in it.

Bacteria Tiny organisms made up of only one cell. Some live inside other organisms. Some types cause disease. Bacteria play a vital role in recycling nutrients in the soil.

Bronchus The tube through which air passes from the trachea to each lung. Inside the lungs, each bronchus subdivides into smaller branches called bronchioles.

Capillaries The smallest type of blood vessels, whose walls are only one cell thick.

Carbohydrates Foods like sugars and starches, which provide energy.

Cartilage A fibrous material, sometimes called gristle. It provides cushioning layers between bones in some joints.

Cell A tiny "building block" which makes up all the tissues in all living things, including plants. A cell is like a miniature factory, producing proteins and many other vital substances.

Chromosome A tiny, thread-shaped body inside the nucleus of a cell. Chromosomes are made of tightly wound strands of DNA and proteins.

Diaphragm The sheet of muscle separating the chest from the abdomen.

DNA (short for deoxyribonucleic acid) A molecule found in chromosomes whose structure encodes an organism's genes.

Embryo The name given to a baby in the first weeks of its development in the uterus.

Enzyme A substance, usually a kind of protein, that speeds up chemical reactions. Enzymes help the body to digest food, and obtain energy from it.

Esophagus The tube through which food passes from the mouth to the stomach.

Evolution The process by which living things have changed over time, gradually adapting to their environment.

Genes The instructions contained in the chromosomes and which are passed from parent to offspring. Because they control the way in which all the cells are built, they determine an organism's characteristics.

Germination The growth of a plant from a seed. Conditions required for germination include a supply of water and oxygen, and a favorable temperature.

Gland An organ that produces a useful substance inside an animal, for example, sweat, saliva, and digestive juices.

Hormones Chemical substances carried in the blood that control various processes. Adrenaline, for example, makes the heart beat faster.

Intestine The tube linking the stomach to the rectum. The first part, called the small intestine, takes in nutrients from the digested food. The second part, the colon or large intestine, leads waste to the rectum.

Ligament A strong, fibrous strap that holds bones together at a joint.

Moneran An organism that is made up of a single cell without a nucleus. Bacteria are monerans.

Nephron Microscopic filtering unit found in the kidney that removes waste substances and excess water from the blood.

Neuron A nerve cell. It carries messages to or from the brain.

GLOSSARY

Nutrients Raw materials that an organism must obtain in order to make and repair its body. For humans, nutrient are: proteins, carbohydrates, fats, vitamins, and minerals.

Organ A structure made of different kinds of cells which does a particular job in the body. The brain, stomach, thyroid gland, and skin are all examples of organs.

Organism Any living thing.

Ovary The female reproductive organ which produces eggs.

Pancreas An organ which produces digestive enzymes and releases them into the intestine. It also produces the hormones insulin and glucagon which control the levels of sugar in the blood.

Pelvis The ring of bones at the base of the spinal column onto which the leg bones are joined (also known as the hip bone).

Peristalsis The squeezing action in the esophagus, stomach, and intestines which pushes the food along.

Photosynthesis The process by which green plants use sunlight as an energy source to turn carbon dioxide and water into the sugars they need for food. A chemical called chlorophyll, found in cells in a plant's leaves, absorbs the sunlight and begins the process.

Pituitary gland An organ situated at the base of the brain which controls the production of hormones.

Pollination The transfer of pollen, tiny particles containing a male cell, from the male part of a plant to a female one.

Predator An animal that obtains its food by hunting and attacking other animals.

Proteins Chemical substances found in all organisms that carry out many essential tasks. For example, in humans, they form enzymes, which allow chemical processes to take place; they make up other substances that protect against diseases; they are found in muscles, skin, and cartilage.

Protist An organism that is made up of a single cell containing a nucleus.

Retina The layer of light-sensitive cells in the back of the eye.

Spinal cord The thick bunch of nerves that run from the brain down the back of the body.

Spore A minute particle produced by plants, bacteria and fungi, from which a new organism can grow.

Tendon A strong fibrous cord that attaches a muscle to a bone.

Testis The male reproductive organ which produces sperm, special cells that can fertilize a female egg.

Trachea The tube, sometimes called the windpipe, which connects the lungs to the mouth and nose.

Ureter The tube through which urine passes from the kidneys to the bladder.

Urethra The tube through which urine passes from the bladder to outside the body.

Uterus Also called the womb, an organ which is connected to the ovaries by tubes. If an egg has been fertilized it will attach itself to the uterus wall and there develop into an embryo and eventually a baby.

Vein A tube which carries blood to the heart. Most carry blood drained of oxygen but the pulmonary veins, which run from the lungs to the heart, carry blood with fresh oxygen in it.

Vertebra One of a chain of bones that make up the backbone, or spinal column.

Villi Tiny, fingerlike projections. The inside of the small intestine is lined with villi.

Virus A microscopic, disease-carrying organism that can only reproduce itself inside the cell of a living organism.

Vitamin An essential chemical that the body needs, in small amounts, to function properly.

INDEX

Page numbers in **bold** refer to main entries.

A

abdomen 36
actrin 44
adenine 53
adenovirus 9
adrenal gland 32, 51
adrenaline 51, 60
AIDS 9
albatrosses 28
algae 10-11
alveoli 38-39, 60
amnion 56
amniotic fluid 57
amoeba 4, 9
anemia 37
angiosperms
animals 4-5, 6-7, 18-31
   adaptation to environment by 6-7, **24-25**
   behavior in 7, **28-29**
   courtship in 28
   evolution of 6-7
   features of 18
   feeding in **18-19**
   methods of attack by **26**
   methods of defense by **27**
   mouths of 18
   movement in **22-23**
   number of species of 18
   of desert 24
   of ocean 25, 31
   of seashore 25
   polar 25, 30
   senses in **20-21**
   territory of 28
anteater 18
antelopes 23, 27
antennae 21
anther 13
antibody 60
anus 19, 36
anvil bone 50
aorta 40, 41
appendix 32
armadillos 27
arteries 33, 36, 40-41, 60
   pulmonary 38, 40, 60
atria, heart 40
auditory nerve 50
auditory ossicles 50
axon 49

B

baby, development of 55, **56-57**
bacilli 8
backbone 47
bacteria 5, 8, 9, 41, 58, 60
barnacles 22
bat, vampire 18
bats 21, 22-23
bean 15
beetle
   great diving 19
   harlequin longhorn 21
beetles 4, 23, 27
biceps 42, 44
bile 35
bird of paradise 7
birds 18, 22-23, 28, 30
birds, flight in 22-23
birth canal *see* vagina
bladder 32, 36, 54
blastocyst 55
blood 36, 39, 40, **41,** 45, 46, 51, 52, 56, 58, 60-61
blood cells 46, 52
   red 41
   white 8, 41
blubber 25
bone fractures 47, 58
bones 42-43, 44-45, **46-47,** 60
brackets 15
brain 32, **48-49,** 52, 56, 59
brain stem 48
breathing **38-39**
broad-leaves 16-17
bronchioles 33, 38, 60
bronchus 33, 38, 60
bryophytes 10
buttercup 11
butterflies 27
butterfly, monarch 30-31

C

camels 24
camouflage 24, 27
cancer 58
canines 34
capillaries 36, 38, 41, 60
carbohydrates 37, 60
carbon dioxide 12, 16-17, 39, 60-61
cardiologist 59
caribou 30-31
carnivores 19, 26-27
carpals 42
cartilage 32, 39, 47, 60
cat, domestic 20
caterpillars 27
catfish 21
cell division 55
cell membrane 8, 52
cells 5, 9, 12-13, 14, 18, 32, 37, 41, 49, 51, **52-53,** 54-55, 60-61
cerebellum 48
cerebral cortex 48
cerebrum 48
cervix 33, 54
chameleon 26
cheetah 23
chemosenses 21
chemotherapy 58
cherry 14
chlorophyll 12, 61
chloroplasts 12
chorion 56
chromosomes 52, 55, 60
chyme 35
cilia 39
circulatory system 32, 40-41
clavicle 42
cocci 8
coccyx 42
cochlea 50
Coelophysis 4
colon 60
colugo (flying lemur) 22
comet 5
common cold 9, 58
cones 16
conifers 10-11, 16
cornea 50
costal nerve 49
cotyledons 11, 15
crab, hermit 29
cranial nerve 9
cranium 42-43
cricket, bush 27
crocus 11
cucumber 14
cytoplasm 8, 52
cytosine 53

D

deer 19, 23, 27
deltoid 42-43
dendrites 49
dentine 34
dermis 45
desert life 24
detritivores 19
diaphragm 33, 38
dicotyledons 11
digestion 18-19, **34-35, 36,** 37
digestive sytem 34, 36, 37
dinosaurs 4, 6
disease 8-9, 58, 60
DNA 8-9, 52-53, 55, 60
doctors 59
dog, domestic 21
dolphins 22
dragonfly 19

E

ear 32, 50
Earth, formation of 5
echolocation 21
eel, European 30-31
electricity, ability to sense 21
electrosenses 21
elephant, African 7
elephants 6-7, 27
elephant-snout fish 21
embryo 7, 55, 56, 60
emu 30
enamel 34
endocrine system 51
endoplasmic reticulum 52
energy 4-5, 10, 12, 34, 37, 38, 60
enzymes 35, 60-61
epidermis 45
epididymis 54
epiglottis 35, 39
epithelium 36
esophagus 35, 39, 61
evolution **6-7,** 24, 60
eyes 20, 32, 50, 61
   compound 20

F

falcon, peregrine 23
fallopian tubes 33, 54
fats (lipids) 37, 61
femur 42, 46
ferns 10-11
fetus 56
fiber 37
fibrils 44
fibula 42
filament 13
finches, Hawaiian 6
fingers, development of 57
fish 27, 29
fish, movement in 22-23

62

INDEX

flagellum 8
flamingo 18
flowers 11,13
flu *see* influenza 9
fly 21
flying fish 27
flying lemur *see* colugo
fly, tsetse 20
follicles, hair 45
foraminiferans 9
fossils 6
frog, water-holding 24
frogs 18
fruits **14-15**
fungi 5, **15**
   life cycle of 15

G

gall bladder 32, 35
gazelles 23, 27
gecko 24
genes 8, 28, 32, **52-53**, 55, 58, 60
gerbils 24
germination 60
glands 51, 60
glucose 52
gluteus maximus 43, 44
gnu *see* wildebeest
Gomphotherium 7
gorilla 23
guanine 53
gymnosperms 10

H

hammer bone 50
hawkmoth 18
hazel 14
hearing 20, 48, 50
heart 33, **40,** 41, 55, 56, 59, 60
heartwood 16
hedgehogs 27
herbivores 19
hemophilia 58
hip bone 33, 47
hip joint 46-47
hormones 48, 51, 54, 60-61
human beings 4, 6
human body **32-33,** 34-57, 58, 60-61
Human Immuno-deficiency Virus (HIV) 9
humerus 42
hummingbirds 23
hyoid bone 33
hyphae 15
hypothalamus 48

I

immunization 58
incisors 34
influenza (flu) 9
insects 22
   flight in 23
insulin 61
intensive care 59
intestines 19, 32, 35, 36, 37, 60
iris 50

J

jawbone 34
jay 14
Jenner, Edward 58
jerboa, long-eared 24
jerboas 24
joints **46-47**

K

kangaroos 30
kelp, giant 10
kidneys 32, 36, 60
killer whale *see* orca
knee joint 46-47

L

ladybug 4
larynx (voice box) 33, 39
leaves 10, 12, 16-17,
lens 50
life
   definition of **4-5**
   origins of 5
ligaments 47, 60
lions 29
lipids *see* fats
lips 34
liver 32, 34-35, 36, 41
liverworts 10-11
lizards 27
locust desert 30-31
louse, head 19
lungs 33, 38-39, 60

M

macrophages 41
magnolia 11
malaria 9
mammoth 6-7
mandible 42
mantis 26
   pink orchid 6
maple 14
marrow, bone 46
mayfly 19
medicine **58-59**
meerkat 29
menstrual cycle 54-55
metacarpals 42
metatarsals 42
migration 21, **30-31**
mildews 15
minerals 37, 46, 61
mistletoe 19
mitochondria 52
Moeritherium 6
molars 34
molds 15
mole 20
monerans 5, 8, 60
monkey, howler 28
monkeys 23
monocotyledons 11
morula 55
mosses 10-11
moth, burnet 27
moths 20-21, 27
mouth 34
movement 44-45, 48
mucus 39
muscles 38-39, 40-41, **42-43, 44-45,** 49, 50-51, 52, 57
mushrooms 15
musk oxen 25, 27
mussels 22
mycelium 15
myosin 44

N

nasal cavity 39, 51
natural selection 7
nectar 13, 18
nephrons 36, 60
nerves 20, 45, 48-49, 50-51, 52, 59, 60-61
nervous system 49, 51
neurologist 59
neuron 48, 60
nucleotides 53
nucleus, cell 52, 55
nurses 59
nutrients 10, 12, 15, 18-19, 36, **37,** 55, 56-57, 60
   recycling of 8, 15
nuts 14

O

oil gland 45
olfactory area 51
olfactory nerve 51
ommatidia 20
omnivores 19
operating theater 59
opossum, honey 13
optic nerve 50
orange 14
orangutan 23
orbicularis oculi 42, 45
orbicularis oris 42, 45
orca (killer whale) 29
orchids 14
organelles 52
organisms 61
   classification of 5
   features of 4
   microscopic 4-5, 8
   prehistoric 4-5, 6
organs 56, 61
ovary 13, 33, 51, 54, 61
oviduct 54
ovules 13
ovum 55
owl
   snowy 25
   tawny 26
owls 20, 26
oxygen 12, 16, 38-39, 40, 48, 57, 60

P

Palaeomastodon 6
paleontology 6
palisade cells 12
pancreas 32, 35, 51, 61
panda, giant 4
papillae 51
parasites 15, 19
patella 42
peas 14
pelvis 42-43, 61
penguins 22, 25
penis 54
peristalsis 35, 61
petal 13
phloem 16
photosynthesis 10, 12, 61
phytoplankton 10
pinna 50
pituitary gland 32, 48, 51, 61
placenta 56-57
plankton 10
plants 5
plants **10-11,** 12-17
   asexual reproduction in 15
   classification of 10
   evolution of 11
   features of 10, 12-13
   flowering 11, 13, 14-15, 16-17
   germination of 15
   life processes of 10, **12-13**

63

INDEX

nonflowering 10
nutrition 12
  parts of 12-13
  reproduction in 13
  vascular 10
plasma 41
plasmodia 9
platelets 41
Pleurococcus 10
poison 26-27
polar bear 25
pollen 13, 61
pollination 13, 61
pondweeds 10
porcupine fish 27
porcupines 27
predators 6, 19, 24, 26, 61
pregnancy 56
prehensile tails 23
premolars 34
prostate gland 54
proteins 9, 37, 44, 52, 60-61
protists 5, **9,** 10, 61
ptarmigan 25
pteridophytes 10
puberty 54
pubic symphysis 47
puffer fish 27
pulp 34
pupil 50
python 26

R

radiolarians 9
radius 42
rafflesia 15
rattlesnake 26
rays 21
rectum 35, 60
reflex action 49
reproduction 4, 13, 14, 15, 53, **54-55**
reproductive system
  female 54
  male 54
respiratory system 38
retina 50, 61
ribs 42-43
roots (of plant) 12, 16-17
ruminants 19

S

sacrum 42-43, 47
salamander, cave 20
saliva 34
salivary glands 33
salmon 31
sapwood 16-17

scapula 43
sciatic nerve 49
scrotum 54
sea anemone 29
sea cucumber 25
seals 25
sea slug 27
seaweeds 10-11
seeds 11, **14-15**
  dispersal of 14
semicircular canals 50
seminal vesicle 54
senses 20-21, **50-51**
sex organs (in humans) 54
sexual intercourse 54-55
sexual selection 7
sharks 6, 21, 22
shark, tiger 22
shellfish 25
sidewinder 24
sight 20, 48, 50
skeleton 32, **42-43,** 46-47
skin **45**
skull 42-43, 47
sloths 23
smallpox 58
smell 21, 51
snails 27
snakes 23, 26
soil 8
speech 39, 48
sperm 54-55
spermatozoon 55
sperm duct 54
spiders 26
spinal cord 48-49, 56, 61
spine 47
spirilli 8
spirogyra 10
spleen 32
spores 10, 15, 61
squirrels 14, 23
stapedius 44
stem 10, 12
sternum 42
stigma 13
stirrup bone 44, 50
stomach 19, 32, 35, 37
stomata 12
strawberry plant 14
style 13
sunflower seeds 14, 37
surgery 58
suture joint 46-47
sweat gland 45
sweet chestnut 14
symbiosis 29
synovial fluid 47

T

tapeworm 18
tarsals 42
taste 21, 48, 51
taste buds 51
teeth 33, 34-35
tendon 44, 61
tern, Arctic 30
testis 51, 54, 61
thalamus 48
thallus 10
throat 35, 38-39
thymine 53
thymus gland 33, 51
thyroid gland 33, 51
tibia 42
tibial nerve 49
tiger 18-19
toads 27
toadstools 15
tongue 33, 34-35
tonsils 33
tortoises 27
touch 48-49
trachea 33-39, 60-61
trapezius 42-43
tree
  banyan 17
  Douglas fir 17
  horse chestnut 17
  ironwood 15
  palm 11, 16
  sequoia, giant 4, 11
trees **16-17**
  deciduous 16
  evergreen 16
  features of 16
  internal layers of 16
  yearly cycle of 17
triceps 42-43, 44
turtle, green 31
turtles 6, 27
twins 53

U

ulna 42
umbilical cord 57
ureter 32, 36, 61
urethra 33, 54, 61
urine 36
uterus (womb) 33, 54-55, 56-57, 60-61
uvula 33

V

vaccination 58
vagina (birth canal) 33, 54, 57
valves, heart 40

vein
  pulmonary 38, 40, 61
veins 33, 36, 41, 61
vena cava 40-41
ventricles, heart 40
Venus flytrap 12
vertebrae 42-43, 47, 56, 61
villi 36, 61
viruses **9,** 41, 58, 60-61
vitamins 37, 61
vitreous humor 50
vocal cords 39
voice box *see* larynx
vomiting 35

W

walnut 14
walrus 25
warthogs 27
whale,
  gray 31
  killer *see* orca
whales 18, 25
wild dogs 29
wild boar 27
wildebeest (gnu) 30
wolves 27, 29, 31
womb *see* uterus
wrasse 29

XYZ

xylem 16
yak 25
yeasts 15
yolk sac 56
zebras 27
zooplankton 10